DONKEY

Indian Wild Asses in the Rann of Kutch [*Photo " The Field"*

DONKEY

The Story of the Ass from East to West

by Anthony Dent

Foreword by R. S. SUMMERHAYS

GEORGE G. HARRAP & CO. LTD

London   Toronto   Wellington   Sydney

Do not call your brother an ass,
for you are the next of kin.

Maltese proverb

First published in Great Britain 1972
by GEORGE G. HARRAP & CO. LTD
182–184 High Holborn, London WC1V 7AX

ISBN 0 245 59932 0

m 8406/591

Composed in Linotype Caledonia and
printed by William Clowes & Sons, Limited
London, Beccles and Colchester
Made in Great Britain

Foreword

THE antiquity of the Ass is very great and undisputed, and the world's literature is packed with references to the Ass, the Donkey, the Mule, or any other of the many names by which it has been known. It was not, however, until recent times that the donkey, unlike the horse, enjoyed the advantage of having books devoted solely to its breeding, training, and welfare, all of which have sought to advise and satisfy the needs of the hordes of owners who have fallen to its charms. No doubt these have been, and are, serving a very useful purpose.

No practical advice of this sort, however, will be found in this most excellent book of Anthony Dent's, no word of help to the puzzled owner of this lovable animal; instead he tells us at considerable length and in great detail the fascinating story of the humble ass throughout the ages, much too of that strange, greatly misunderstood, yet to many of us much to be admired, relative, the Mule.

Many facts and countless figures can well make very dull reading, especially when offered at book-length, yet, reading this book, I find myself fascinated by the story of the donkey, by the charm and humour with which it is told, and frankly somewhat bewildered by the author's exceptional diligence and erudition. One gets the impression that Anthony Dent has searched every corner of the earth to tell us about all there is to be known of the donkey, and during his journey collected many intriguing and unusual drawings to embellish this outstanding work.

Having as it were enriched the earth to tell us of the various types and where to find them, he ends up in Ceylon, where donkeys, we learn, are few in number. The donkey of Ceylon, he writes, "is a dwarf, but a comely dwarf, of charming proportions, an attractive dark-brown, almost coffee-coloured. All donkey foals are enchanting, but the Ceylonese especially so with their thimble-sized hoofs and large round eyes. If anyone had designed a plush toy, in this shape, with this colour and texture of coat, you would say it was unreal and sentimental. But no. It seems God can be sentimental too, sometimes." Of course every donkey-lover should read this book—and share my enjoyment, which has been great. Here is surely the Complete Story of the Donkey.

R. S. SUMMERHAYS

Contents

Illustrations

Prologue

THE WORDS

THE MUSIC, of course, has been the same since the dawn of history and before. For though one of the consequences of domestication is sometimes that the domestic animal comes to make a different sound from its wild ancestor (for instance, neither the wolf nor the jackal barks, and dogs do not howl in quite the same way as their wild cousins do), the tame ass makes the same melodious (the word is George Washington's description) utterance as its now very rare wild prototype in the Nubian desert.

The word 'donkey' is peculiar to the English language in the sense that no related word with the same meaning occurs in any modern European tongue, though it is probable that it was derived from a Flemish word. Until recently it rhymed with 'monkey' throughout most of England, and was so pronounced in upper-class speech until about 1850; this pronunciation is still in use throughout Ireland, and in some English dialects. The word monkey was probably first applied to specimens of the capuchin ape, and was derived from a Flemish word *monnekijn*, which means 'a little monk', harping on the monastic appearance of that species. The most likely origin of 'donkey' is similar, from a Flemish word *donnekijn*, meaning a small dun-coloured animal. Now, all these Flemish borrowings—of which there are a fair number in English—can be traced to a fairly brief period about the fourteenth century, and if the English word 'donkey' really goes back as far as that—to Chaucer's lifetime, say—it is remarkable that no written instance of it survives before 1785, when it appears as an entry in the *Dictionary of the Vulgar Tongue*, by Francis Grose. Grose was an Army officer married to an actress, but his lexicon is not exclusively a glossary of barrack-room slang, or of green-room argot, though both these and the vernacular of the officer's mess are found in it. Some of it is very vulgar indeed, and it forms a rich treasury of the talk of cadgers and card-sharpers, horse-thieves and highwaymen

and harlots, pimps and poufs and ponces in their habit as they
lived in Georgian England. This would mean that the word
donkey had had an underground existence of about four hundred years in English, which is remarkable, but not impossible
or without precedent. Grose adds a few slang synonyms—not as
many as one would expect—the most striking being "The King
of Spain's Trumpeter", on which he enlarges, because in his
view donkey was derived from Don, meaning a Spaniard. He is
almost certainly wrong.

His contemporary Dr Johnson does not record the word at
all. He died the year before Grose's book was published, and
his omission is sufficient indication that educated opinion in
England would agree with the Great Cham of Fleet Street, that
the only proper designation of this animal was *ass*. At this time,
and certainly in Johnson's Staffordshire mouth, the pronunciation with a long a was no longer in favour outside Ireland,
where it is still current. One hears it still in certain English
circles,[1] though almost always metaphorically and almost always
in the combination 'silly ass'. To me its associations are purely
anatomical; but such is the mutability of phonetics in English
on either side of the Atlantic that when an American talks of
'sitting on his ass' he does not mean mounted on a donkey. Or,
as Patton said to Eisenhower:

> "Get off your ass
> Send up the gas"

What we may therefore regard as the standard English ren-
dering of what the zoologist calls *Equus asinus* is by no means
of mysterious origin. It is part of a long chain of names in
various languages for an animal, adopted in the same order as
the speakers of various languages became acquainted with it,
and reaching back far into the past. Only the first link in the
chain is missing. We do not know what word was employed for
ass by its original Berber or Hamitic masters. But the 'second
owners', the Semitic peoples, called it *anah*,[2] feminine *anoth*,
and from this the Greek word *onos* is derived. From this is taken
on the one hand the Latin *asinus*, and its later derivatives such

---

[1] Usually those which employ the genteel Cockneyisms 'gorn orf', and
'orfen'.

[2] Modern Arabic *hamar*, Maltese *hmar*.

as the French *âne*, etc., and on the other *asal* or something very
like it in the Celtic language of the Gauls. The word *asal* was
current in Old Irish, though the donkey was not seen in Ireland
until after the language had ceased to be spoken in its archaic
form. From the Celtic languages the Germanic peoples bor-
rowed the word, and it appears typically in the West Germanic
(including Anglo-Saxon) *esol*, from which the Slavonic words
such as *osel* are derived. In terms, therefore, of European languages the usual form is upset. Because most of the domestic
animals that we know today were present in the homeland of
the Indo-European language group before the great dispersal
from the Transcaspian heartland of the Aryans which began
four thousand years ago, words or synonyms, related collater-
ally, are found throughout the language group for such con-
cepts as Horse, Swine, Ox, Goat; but because they are not
derived from each other but from a remote common ancestor
their family resemblance is by now minimal. Not so with the
unique Ass, which as we shall see was not native to the region
where the Indo-European languages had their birth, and which
had not been introduced there when the inhabitants of the
region were dispersed. And if in a sense the tidal flow of the
word ass seems to run contrary to the sub-title of this essay
(for reasons which will become apparent below), nevertheless
over a long stretch of the way the currents do run parallel,
because the Greeks did borrow the animal and the word from
the Semites, the Romans from the Greeks, the Celts from the
Romans, the Goths (who called it *asilus*) also from the Romans,
the West Germanic peoples from the Goths, and finally the
Slavs from the Germans.

The diminutives and slang pet names for the ass in English
are legion, and most of them will be explained in the course of
later chapters, but there is one that has long defied interpretation. This is Moke. It did not appear in print until after Donkey
—not until 1840, in fact, when it was still often spelt Moak.
Eric Partridge explains that it has no connection with any of
the foregoing, and that we owe it to the Gipsies. One might
have guessed that they would be involved in the affair sooner
or later! Specifically to the Welsh Gipsies, in whose language
mokhio means an ass. This Welsh Gipsy term is derived from
the general Romany word *moila* or *meila*, having the same

meaning as, and probably going back to, the Latin word *mulus*, for the interpretation of which no prize is offered. How and when the transfer of meaning from 'mule' to 'ass' took place we shall never know, but two explanations are possible. It might be part of the general gipsy pattern, whereby the merchandise is made to appear more attractive by calling it by the name of something bigger; in the same way as gipsy horse-dealers (well, partly horse-dealers) 'talked up' the stallion-jenny hybrid by calling it a jennet instead of a hinny, thus applying to it the name of a stamp of pacing pony formerly much esteemed in England, so that they may have blinded the gorgios with science now and again by offering for sale what they called mules, but which to the ignorant eye might appear to be nothing more than asses. It may be the legacy of such gifted sales-talk, or it may be a memory of the sudden depression in their standard of living which many gipsy tribes undoubtedly experienced after first coming to Britain. At times many of them were exclusively to be found—even in the New Forest area, where their lives were relatively secure and prosperous—without vans or carts of any kind, moving all their worldly goods by pack-saddle on donkeys alone, and living in benders. But in some of the countries where they had lived the gipsies were acknowledged mule experts—as in Spain, for instance—and it may be that they came to apply the word *meilo* to what was for the moment all the mule they had. There are precedents for such a development. Certainly by the time the Gipsy name for Doncaster—Meilo-gav—became current among them the word *meilo* must have connoted only 'ass'; Meilo-gav, literally 'Donkey-town', is a pun on the first element (Donc—) in the English name of a place important to the travelling people both as a road-centre and as a horse-racing venue.

Although each European language has relatively few alternative words, beyond the bare essentials to distinguish male from female, young from adult asses, and even then tends to borrow from the vocabulary of the horse, Semitic languages have a wealth of such words, the reason being simply that the daily lives of the Semitic peoples were for so long and so intensively concerned with donkey business that they needed a large technical vocabulary. Thus the Old Semitic word *anah* quoted above was the commonest, and least specialized, of the words used. An almost equally common expression, in the Hebrew of the Old Testament, was *hamor*, meaning a working ass; and this is the same word as the modern Arabic *hamal* = porter, which nicely defines the function of the ass in Near Eastern life. The word used by Job, on the other hand, to mean the wild ass or onager, is *pere* (also applied in Genesis to the desert migrant Ishmael), which is derived from a verb meaning 'to run'. The implications of these two words would serve of themselves to define the differences between Neddy and his wild relatives which are the subject of our opening chapter.

1 *The Brothers of the Ass*

Wounded ass, from cave drawing near Santander, Spain

THIS is the earliest European picture of a donkey, drawn on the wall of a cave at El Castillo, near Santander, in Spain. It is dying of arrow-wounds, for the hunting peoples of the Old Stone Age had no domestic animals (except perhaps dogs), and to them the horse and the ass and the cow were simply game animals like the deer and the elk. Of the large grass-eating animals in this Europe of long ago, the donkey was among the least common—indeed, it was really an overspill from the African animal world, just as the only European monkeys, the

Barbary Apes of Gibraltar, really belong to Africa; no one knows
how and when the first of either species crossed the Straits into
Europe, but these straits are after all much narrower than the
Strait of Dover, and there was a time when there was a solid
land bridge between Morocco and Spain. Even with the water
at its present extent, both the ape and the ass are strong enough
swimmers to have kept afloat long enough for the right combination of wind, tide, and current to have swept them from
continent to continent if they had been chased into the water
(say by lions) on the African shore at the ebb-tide.

    These wild asses, then, were never very numerous or wide-
spread in Europe, but they do belong to the variety which later
became the ancestor of the domestic donkey, for it is quite
certainly to Africa that we owe this addition to the group of
auxiliary creatures by whose aid man began his conquest of
the world, beginning with the growing of crops and the building of towns. Whereas the ancestors of the horse and the camel
until the very latest stage of their evolution lived in America,

Two Nubian wild jennies, Wadi Sharag, Sudan
| *Mrs Michael Mason*

and wandered into Asia not long (geologically speaking) before the land bridge over the North Pacific Ocean broke down, all animals recognizable from their fossil remains as asses belonged exclusively to the Old World. And whereas only one (or at the very most two) species of wild horse exists, or has existed, from which tame horses can trace their descent, there are more than half a dozen distinct races of wild ass living in the world today, and there have been more within historical memory. The wild asses fall into two distinct groups, Asiatic and African, of which the former are often loosely called onagers, and bear the pseudo-Greek name Hemionus in the language of zoologists— a confusing and ill-chosen name because it means 'half an ass', suggesting that it is the result of a cross between an ass and some other creature, whereas what the learned godfathers Sclater, Pallas, Lydekker, and others meant to imply (bless their erudite hearts) was that these animals partook equally of the nature of asses and horses.

The donkey bears the signature of his wild ancestor (or at least of his most important wild ancestor) written across him. Whereas not only wild horses but many varieties of wild ass have a dark streak (called a list or an eel-stripe) running down the spine, usually in the same colour as the mane, only the domestic donkey and the Nubian Wild Ass (*Asinus africanus africanus*) have a streak at right angles to it across the withers and down the shoulder. This 'shoulder cross' does occur very occasionally in dun horses which have an eel-stripe, and much more commonly in a blurred form, like a dark shadow on either shoulder, in blue-dun Highland ponies, where it is very often associated with horizontal stripes on the legs. Domestic donkeys seldom, and Nubian and Asiatic wild asses never, have these, but in addition to the horses mentioned above, the Somali Wild Ass (*Asinus africanus somaliensis*) has them. Evidently they are the vestige of a complete system of stripes covering the whole body, as in the zebras, and may be taken to prove that the common ancestor of all solid-hoofed animals—zebras, horses, asses, and onagers alike—must have been striped: or so Darwin, Ewart, and others surmised. On this account it might be argued that the zebras are the most 'primitive', since they alone retain this ancestral feature invariably and in full. But this may simply mean that the conditions which make a striped

coat desirable (that is, aid survival) have lasted longer in the
history of the zebras than in that of the horses or asses. On the
other hand, zebras share with asses, both wild and tame, the
peculiarity of 'chestnuts' (horny excrescences on the inside of
the limbs) on the forelegs only. These are probably vestiges of
the toes which the common ancestor had on all four legs at a
time when it lived in marshy country. The horse still has chestnuts both before and behind; is it therefore more primitive, or
is it simply that the ancestors of zebras and asses have lived
longer in more arid climates than horses, and have 'forgotten'
the necessary conditions of survival in the marshlands? Another
'primitive' characteristic is held by some to be large, long ears.
By this standard the asses of Africa—and hence the domestic
donkey—are the most old-fashioned; next come the Asiatic
asses, zebras and horses having the shortest ears, while those of
all zebra species are rounded at the tips and the ears of horses
and asses come to a point. None of these characteristics, therefore, add up to an indication of how early the various species
now living branched off from the common stock of solid-hoofed
mammals, or in what order.

Because, as we shall see later, there is some reason to believe
that our donkey is not descended exclusively from one wild
species alone, it is worth while to look briefly at all the kinds
of wild ass existing in the present and the known past, both the
African and the Asiatic groups. As late as Roman times there
were wild asses all across Northern Africa, from the Horn of
Somaliland to the Atlantic coast of Morocco. The northern limit
—somewhere about the frontier of Kenya with Somalia and
Ethiopia—of Grant's Zebra is also the southern limit of the
Somali Wild Ass, and illustrates a general rule that only the
territories of the several species of zebra overlap at all—otherwise, where one species ends the other begins. The Somali
Wild Ass grows to about fourteen hands high and is reddish-
grey in colour, with occasional horizontal dark markings on the
legs. Otherwise the legs are light-coloured, as with all wild
asses (whereas wild horses all have black legs ('points') from
the knee downward). A dwarf variety of the Somali is found
on the island of Socotra.

Between the edge of the Sahara Desert and the south shore
of the Mediterranean was the domain of the Nubian Wild Ass,

now very rare. Wild asses in the west of the Atlas mountains are now probably descended in part from escaped or abandoned domestic asses, but in ancient times a smaller variety of the Nubian was hunted there (the Mauretania of the Romans), and a mosaic in a Roman villa as far east as Bône, in Algeria, shows a native Numidian horseman riding without saddle or bridle in pursuit of what recognizably is a small Nubian Wild Ass. Even the larger variety does not grow much above twelve hands, and is of an unvarying grey colour, as are most domestic asses, though colour varieties including chocolate brown, reddish brown, white, and parti-coloured occur today among the latter.

The colour scheme of the Asiatic wild asses is quite different. All are wholly or predominantly yellow in tone, they have no shoulder cross, and their ears are not nearly so long as in the African species. An eel-stripe is almost always to be seen. The

Somali Wild Ass near Sardo, Ethiopia, 1970. About five hundred
of this species survive in the wild

[*Photo J. Allan Cash*

area which they now inhabit is much more extensive than the habitat of the African species. It reaches from Syria, Persia, and Iraq in the west right through north central Asia to Siberia, to Mongolia, Kashmir, the high plains of Tibet, and Northern India. It formerly extended farther westward, into Arabia and Asia Minor. In all varieties the white or pale dun colour of the legs and belly is continued upward along the lower part of the neck and the whole face is white, only the forehead being dark. Along the sides the border between the two shades is sharply defined. Behind the shoulder and in front of the thigh the light colour runs up a long way towards the spine. Lightest of all in colour is the Persian race, called the onager in antiquity.

This species has been known to European science since 1756, and a century later the first specimens were brought alive to Paris. They came from somewhere near the Red Sea, where none are found today. Smallest of the Asiatic asses, they grow only to about twelve hands, and have a characteristic dark ring round the coronet (immediately above the hoof).

Since the Asiatic Wild Ass inhabits such a large continuous area, it follows that there should be many local races, such as the Indian, which still lives wild in small bands in the Rann of Kutch. But the differences between these varieties are not all obvious. They depend on size (where one often shades into the other), shape of skull, and niceties of hair-colour (which changes from summer to winter just to make things more difficult), so that only an expert can distinguish between local varieties of onager. The now perhaps extinct Syrian race has shorter ears, which has led scientists to call it *hemippus* ('half horse', as opposed to *hemionus*, 'half ass'—as nice a distinction as that between half full and half empty).

The last important shipment of onagers to Europe was by Karl Hagenbeck of Hamburg in 1954. More than a dozen were captured and brought back after aerial reconnaissance in Northern Persia, and this herd has bred freely in captivity.

Farther east is found the kulan or jigetai, which is on average at least two inches taller than the onager, while the colour of its back is in comparison reddish yellow, and not so deeply indented by white before the thigh and behind the shoulder. The kulan comes from Transcaspia, Turkmenia, Turkestan, North China, Mongolia, South and East Siberia. It runs in mixed herds with antelopes, never with onagers in the West or with wild horses in the East. It is better known to science because its habitat is larger than that of the other races, it is found in greater numbers, and it is not confined to remote, infertile, and arid regions. Nevertheless, it too is being pushed back into the wilderness, under the cunning leadership of tough old stallions, often covered with scars from the duels of the mating season, and away from contact with men and their repeating rifles and their cross-country cars. It will be a long time before the kulan is extinct, however, and on Russian territory at least an intelligent conservation policy has actually led to an increase in numbers. Colour varies somewhat locally; in Transcaspia it is washed-out grey, in North-west India reddish, along the Soviet-Chinese border yellow; in this last region the average height is greater also. Its nose in all regions is blunter, and the whole head, seen from the side, thicker than in the onager.

The kiang of the Pamirs, the Himalayas, and, more particularly, of Tibet, is the largest Asiatic race, standing between thirteen and fourteen hands high, the height of the Somali Ass, which it also resembles in its bright sandy red colour along the back, which forms a greater contrast with its whitish-dun under-parts.

The shape of the head is lumpy, and its appearance heavy. The feet resemble more those of a horse than an ass, the hoof being rounded rather than narrow. There is a thick, woolly winter coat; when this is being changed for the smooth summer coat the kiangs cannot shed the old hairs fast enough, for the transition between the icy winter and the hot summer of the Tibetan mountains is swift, so that they roll on the ground to rub off the winter coat. (The same habit has been observed in the domestic ass.) Outside Tibet, Yarkand and Kashmir are the most important habitat of the kiang, which is not often seen in captivity. There are specimens in the London Zoo, and something of a herd at Hellabrunn, near Munich. The contrast between the reddish-yellow summer coat and the slate-grey, woolly winter coat is more striking than in other races. The kiang lives on hard grasses and the stunted shrubs of the desert. On this diet the animals put on a great deal of fat in summer, so that when they are hunted for meat in the autumn, and the hunters are making soup or stew, they have to skim it many times to get rid of the grease. This layer of fat under the skin is of great service to the kiang as an insulator in cold weather. The Tibetans have managed to tame another weather-proof Himalayan mammal, the Yak, and the same qualities would seem to commend the kiang as a potential draught animal. But all attempts at taming it have failed, and it would probably be useless away from its native mountains, because its respiratory system and probably its blood-pressure have by now been attuned to function at high altitudes only, in a rarified atmosphere at low pressure. The fact that kiangs survive in zoos at sea-level is of no consequence: they are not working; and for the larger grass-eating animals, 'work' means mostly flight from their mortal enemies at top speed for miles on end.

2 Going into Service

THE Eastern Desert of Egypt, the territory lying between the
Nile Valley and the Red Sea, presents a forbidding landscape
today. Dry, treeless, almost stripped of its soil by erosion, it
supports little wild life other than scorpions and desert rats.
Camel caravans cross it only with the greatest difficulty. It is
scored by waterless gullies which are flushed at intervals of
some years by flood waters that rush down to the Nile on
one hand and the Red Sea on the other, leaving behind them
hardly a trace of life-giving moisture until the next rare down-
pour. But five thousand years ago these were rivers running
(or at least trickling) all the year round. There were trees then
on these nightmare hills. In one of these wadis, Abu Wasil in

Rock-drawing by ancient hunters at Wadi Abu Wasil, Eastern
Desert, Upper Egypt, showing bowmen with trapped or tethered
Nubian Asses

southern Upper Egypt, H. A. Winkler, who devoted several years between the World Wars to the exploration of this stony waste, found a highly significant series of pictures drawn on the cliffs.

By careful comparison of these with similar drawings in adjoining countries either side of the Red Sea, by separating out common features which distinguish one group of pictures from another, Winkler worked out a time-scale which placed different generations of artists in order, the last of them belonging to the period just before the Egyptian dynasties began. That means all of the pictures were drawn before 3000 B.C. Around 6000 B.C. the people of Wadi Abu Wasil depict themselves as leading the life partly of hunters and partly of cattle-breeders. And one of the animals which they hunted, like the Old Stone Age people in Spain, was the ass. The clearest of these pictures shows some hunters with double-curved bow and quiver approaching donkeys which have been caught in traps. In another an archer escorted by Saluki dogs is attacking game which includes ostrich, wild ox—and donkeys. The presence of the wild ox must of itself show that the district was then quite well watered, but the ostrich must mean that the desert was not far away. In a sense this fixes the ass as a creature of the borderland between the green grass and the thorny scrubland or true desert: but pressure from its enemies (principally man, as long as it remains wild) will drive it into the latter region, where it can survive for countless generations, as we have seen from the account of the Asiatic wild asses in the last chapter.

Archer and Saluki Hounds hunting Nubian Asses, Wadi Abu Wasil

The kind of trap used shows that the object of capture is not the taming of the animals but their killing for food. It has been identified as a 'treadle' trap, an ingenious contrivance with a wooden spring, used mainly for catching deer by the hoof. While it does catch the animal alive, the latter's chances of release from the trap without damage to the leg are almost nil, even supposing that the leg has not already been lamed by the struggles of the prisoner. Again, the hindquarters of the animals are rounded out with fat, suggesting that the object of the hunt is meat (probably the time is the end of the most abundant grazing season).

It is doubtful whether there are any wild asses in the Eastern Desert today. Those in the picture show by their long ears that they belong to one of the African species, but of course we do not know exactly how these were distributed eight thousand years ago. In our day, Wadi Abu Wasil is within the bounds of the Nubian race's stamping-ground, but those bounds may have shifted over the centuries, and in any case it is not very far from the present northern limit of the Somali Wild Ass. Since the difference between these two varieties is largely a matter of

Eastern invaders with asses towing (or dragging over portage) ships from Red Sea to Nile, Wadi Abu Wasil

[*Egypt Exploration Society*

size and colour, since the picture is in black and white, and since we cannot guess the height of the man to use as a standard for judging the height of the animals, they might be either Nubian or Somali.

This last question, though unanswerable, is of some significance, because these pictures are followed after a short interval (short by the standards of accuracy at our disposal, but still before 3000 B.C., still before the first of the Pharaohs) by others which show donkeys of the same type bearing burdens and driven by men. This is the only place in the world where we have such a 'cartoon serial' of the beginnings of animal servitude. In the wild the herds of the two African species run separately and the animals of one do not breed with those of the other, but such is not the case in captivity. And if asses could be caught and tamed here others could be put to work farther south, nearer the Horn of Africa, where they would certainly be of the Somali kind. And whenever two tribes of donkeymen met, we can be sure that the first item on the agenda would be buying and selling or 'swapping' of donkeys: so that a very early cross between Nubian and Somali is the most probable item in this dim chapter of the African past.

Now the scene shifts a little farther west and south, to the fertile valley of the Nile itself, in the days of the Old Kingdom, and slightly after 3000 B.C. Here is a quite elaborate civilization, based on intensive agriculture and gardening in the Nile mud, but using only one working animal. The horse has not yet appeared on the Egyptian scene, nor will it appear until about 1750 B.C., and then not as a working animal but as a mascot, and the camel is not in evidence either. It was to spread into Africa from Western Asia much later than the horse or the water buffalo, which is to be seen working in present-day Egypt. The only pack and draught animal in Old Kingdom Egypt is the ass. It was used there also as an alternative to the plough ox. If there is some doubt as to whether the first Pharaohs and their subjects got Nubian or Somali asses from their neighbours in the Eastern Desert there is no doubt that the main source of supply from the west was unmixed Nubian. The Berber tribes who then inhabited Libya were subjugated by the Egyptians, and they paid tribute in herds of livestock. There are pictures showing this tribute being counted, and it includes droves of donkeys, which look just like the Egyptian donkey of today. The only loads that were not moved by slave porterage in this first of the Nile empires travelled on donkey-back.

Here again, west of the Nile, we have one highly significant picture drawn on the naked rock in the open, which shows the wild ancestor of the Libyan asses, though it comes from farther west than Libya itself. The barren region in the south of Libya which is called the Fezzan has no natural frontiers, and it merges imperceptibly into the Fezzan of Algeria. There in a gully which is called Wadi Djerat is a rather dramatic picture that has something in common with the hunted and wounded ass of Santander, though it was drawn much later. How much later is hard to tell, because the means of comparison which enabled Winkler to fix the age of the Abu Wasil pictures are not so abundant in this part of the Sahara. By its style and associations, however, the picture must be the work of the hunters who were the first human tenants of the Fezzan, not of the later pastoralists or the rarer hopeful peasants who tried to make a living by growing crops round the oases. Full of life, and the (rather desperate) movement typical of the unknown masters of the 'hunting' school, the picture does not show any trace of harness, and the animal is obviously not working. It is wild, and the picture must have been drawn before 4000 B.C. It must also have been drawn (if it is from life and not memory) in the late winter before the grazing began to revive, for the animal is thin to the point of emaciation, a mere shadow of the Abu Wasil and Santander asses.

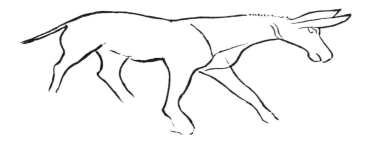

Exhausted Nubian Ass, from rock drawing of pre-pastoral age, Wadi Djerat, Fezzan

Here is the puzzle, for the hunting artists were also magicians. They drew their pictures as magic aids to the hunter; the act of drawing game on the rocks was meant to draw the game within the range of the hunter's arrows. Therefore they drew only fat and fit game. Alternatively, the aim of the magic was to increase the size of the herds, and to this end the artists drew females heavy with young. For instance, the great majority of the horses in European rock paintings are mares visibly in foal. Now, if this donkey is a jenny it is plainly not in foal, and one wonders what can have been the motive in making the picture. Of course, it could have been done by a hunter whose tribal taboos forbade him to eat ass-meat—but in that case, why draw it at all? Maybe this picture is functionless after all, drawn by a man who just *had* to draw, or an original genius who had got bored with turning out the same old pictures, like advertisements for a fatstock show?

The picture does bring out two unmistakable features. The ears, in the characteristic position of exhaustion or stress—as at Santander—are so long that the animal can only belong to the Nubian race, and this painting is almost unique among such early works in showing plainly the shoulder stripe which also spells Nubian. The vigorous portrait shows the scraggy ancestor of the smooth and well-rounded Libyan asses of the tribute pictures.

Since the ears are so prominent in this picture, this might be the appropriate place to hazard an explanation of their great length in the African as compared with the Asiatic races. As mentioned earlier, the ass is a contrary beast, in that it chooses to upset some general zoological rules. For instance, as a general rule, the bigger an animal, the longer the gestation period. In the whale and the elephant it is a matter of years, in the rat it is a matter of weeks, and so on. Yet the ass, which is smaller than the cow or the horse, carries its foal one month longer than does the mare, and three months longer than the cow carries her calf. Mountain races tend to have shorter legs, and cold-dwelling races shorter extremities of all kinds than their near relations on the plains and in warm climates respectively. Typical cold-dwellers have chunky figures (polar bear, musk-ox, seal), typical hot-dwellers long, thin legs (gazelle, antelope). But we have seen that the kiang—which not only lives at a higher altitude but in a colder winter climate than any other wild ass—is higher on the leg than any other of its relatives. But in the matter of ears the ass conforms. The long, trumpet-like ears of the African ass have no acoustic advantage over the shorter, blunter, horse-type ears of the onager, nor do the conditions of life in the two continents make acute hearing any more important in the one than in the other. But then many desert and other hot-zone dwellers have large ears (the object of which is not the better to hear you with, my dear!). Outside the desert, the elephant. In the desert itself, the jerboa or desert rat and the fennec or desert fox. The whole conformation of desert animals is calculated to present the largest possible surface in relation to the total size, and if possible to afford maximum room for sweat glands. This is an aid to cooling by evaporation, and the larger ears of the Nubian ass probably serve the same purpose as the flanges on a motor-cycle engine or on the barrel casing of such machine-guns as the Lewis and the Hotchkiss, which are air-cooled.

Another trend the ass of Africa shares with desert companions is a relatively 'fine' head and sharper muzzle. All the Asiatic varieties have to face at any rate a much colder winter and a shorter summer than do the African, and the kiang, in its high habitat with bitter winters, has the bluntest muzzle and the chunkiest skull of all. The difference in head-shape of asses in Mongolia and the hot deserts is exactly paralleled in terms of the horse. The kertag or Mongolian wild horse has a broad muzzle and a 'thick head', and so had the extinct 'diluvial horse' of Northern Europe, combined with a Roman nose. But the pure-bred Arabian horse of the desert has a tapering skull and a 'dished face' (concave frontal bone) with slender muzzle, only the gristly parts of which round the nostrils fan out when breathing deeply under stress.

After the camel, the African ass is undoubtedly the best performer of all domestic animals under desert conditions, both in its ability to graze and browse on the sparse desert scrub and herbage and in its power to go a long way between drinks. One of the earliest ways in which this ability was exploited was on the desert route which existed in ancient times between the coastal towns of Libya and the upper reaches of the Niger about Timbuktu. Herodotus mentions this route as full of traffic about 500 B.C., but we know it was in fact operating as early as 1200 B.C.; the trade was not in bulk cargoes but in valuable goods in small packets. This was before the days of the camel, and the traffic was two-wheeled chariots with very small bodies—little more than drivers' open cabs or footplates. Pictures of these vehicles drawn by two horses, abound in the Sahara. When in the middle of the Second World War the Colonne Leclerc crossed the desert from Lake Chad, in French West Africa, by a route parallel to this "Way of the Chariots" to attack the Germans on the Libyan front, it was acclaimed as a great feat—in the days of the petrol engine and friendly surveillance from the air. But the horses in the chariot teams consumed more water than the radiators of Leclerc's trucks, proportionately. And they were supplied, at the stages which

Asiatic Nomads at Egyptian border post: tomb painting from Beni Hassan, Egypt, Hyksos period. The Sulaib bedouin of Arabia, horseless and camel-less, preserved this essentially ass-based culture until our own day

[Egypt Exploration Society

had no water-hole, from dumps of water-skins or jars which were carried along the Way of the Chariots under the bellies, rather than on the backs, of strings of asses. Slung in this way, the water did not evaporate so fast through the pores of the skin bottles, being shielded from the direct rays of the sun by the asses' bodies.

The purpose for which men first domesticated the ass will probably now remain for ever unknown to us. But as evidence accumulates—in a region far removed from the homeland of the ass—showing that the first horse-breeders kept only mares, for milk and for the meat of foals, so the analogy that donkeys may have been kept originally to the same end becomes more and more plausible.

Whatever may have been the primary purpose of men in domesticating some work animals, there is no doubt of the purpose in the case of the ass. Since the ass was tamed before the invention of the wheel, and before riding was first heard of (but within the region where the ox was available for ploughing), the work intended can only have been pack-carrying. While this was useful to the sedentary Egyptian farmers, a pack-animal was even more of a blessing to the wandering shepherds and cattlemen on either side of the Nile. Sheep and goats, mainly bred in Sinai and points east, are too small to be effective load-carriers. Cattle, bred by the North African tribes, though in steadily diminishing numbers as the land began to dry out and the Sahara to extend its bounds and become more forbidding, were simply not used for loads. Why this is so is one of the mysteries of prehistory, because it is quite possible to train oxen to carry loads, and when the white men first came to South Africa they found the Hottentots—who were at about the same level of culture as the Berbers of North Africa in Old Kingdom times—using oxen to carry packs, and even for riding.

Owing to the sparseness of grazing in the Near East even in those days, people who depended on stock-herding for a living had to follow the herds not only from one water-hole to the next but from one patch of edible herbage (it would hardly rank as grass by our standards) to another. In this respect they were little better off than the hunters of an earlier age, who had had to migrate in the wake of the large grazing animals which they hunted and killed for a living. To do this on foot, season after

season, carrying clothes, weapons, tools, bedding, tents, food,
and water, was a very wearing occupation. A pint of pure water
weighs a pound and a quarter, and a pint does not last you very
long in the North African summer. To load all those on to the
ass, especially the water, was a liberation from servitude for
the dismounted nomad. There are very few people who live like
this nowadays, but some idea of what it was all like is afforded
by the Masai of Kenya, some of whom still depend solely on
cattle as their form of wealth and have asses as their only means
of transport. (Incidentally, these Masai donkeys may possibly
be dwarf descendants of the Somali Wild Ass.)

The other great river-valley empires of the Old World grew
up in the Indus basin and along the twin rivers of Iraq, the
Tigris and the Euphrates. In the latter region the first people
who have left intelligible records are the Sumerians, with their
capital at Ur. They had ox-drawn sledges from a very early
time, but also around 3000 B.C. they had war-chariots, shown on
the famous "Standard of Ur" in the British Museum apparently
as four-wheeled carts. These are drawn by what appear to be
onagers, and a fragment of harness from Ur consists of a terret
or rein-ring ornamented by a little bronze figure of what can
only be an onager. This is almost the only known example of
the regular use of tame onagers for draught: the experiment
was a blind alley, and we do not know why it was given up.
The usual explanation is that the onager was replaced by the
horse when the latter was introduced into Mesopotamia from
the north in due course, and that the horse also proved the

The Standard of Ur, showing in lowest register teams of
Asiatic wild asses (onagers) ready for harnessing
[*British Museum*

more suitable for military purposes (the onager having been used, so far as we know, only for warfare). But this did not happen until about 2000 B.C. at the earliest—long enough for domestic asses to have reached Ur from Egypt, and for crosses to have been produced between them and the onagers. Here it is worth noting that although the mule, or cross between the horse and both Asiatic and African wild ass, is infertile, that between the two kinds of wild ass is capable of breeding further generations. It is therefore quite possible that during the second millennium B.C. the domestic ass of Iraq and adjacent regions such as Syria and Asia Minor received an infusion of onager blood. The explanation why the pure-bred onager was given up is not quite satisfactory as generally stated. There is another possible reason. It will be seen from the last chapter that wild asses in general, but especially the Asiatic ones, are bigger and taller according to the height at which they live—the Himalayan kiang being the tallest of all. It may well be that the Sumerians breeding onagers obtained in the first place from the Persian highlands found that after some generations in the Valley of the Two Rivers the size decreased, despite selective mating and body-building food. This is a factor that would not operate in the case of the horse (mountain horses are in fact less tall than lowland horses), and may well have led to the replacement of onagers by horses.

Outside Iraq the only pictures of onagers working are in the magnificent wall paintings in the tombs of Thebes, where in one fresco a chariot drawn by skewbald horses of Arab type is shown together with another team of thin-maned, thin-tailed dun animals which are either onagers or mules out of onager mares. But this Egyptian picture is quite late, belonging to New Kingdom times, when so far as we know the tame onager was a thing of the past in Mesopotamia. Probably the beast was just a freak, since the Egyptian kings were great fanciers of rare animals (indeed, the first Zoo proprietors in the world). But even so, the puzzle remains as to where these animals came from—probably farther afield still. Although there are no pictures of comparable date, we do have a single mention by the historian Herodotus to the effect that much later when the Persian army under Xerxes invaded Europe there were within its ranks some chariots drawn by onagers. So it is just possible

Chariot team of onagers (or mules by onager stallions),
from Theban tomb painting

[*British Museum*

Libyan asses brought as tribute to Egypt, getting in the
barley harvest

[*British Museum*

that the Egyptians could have obtained an onager team, ready broken to harness, as a gift from some king in Persia, or in the lands between it and Egypt.

However, all over the East the ass has always taken second place as draught animal to the pack-ass, and even to the riding-ass, and for thousands of years the nomad tribes between Sinai and the Euphrates carried all their moveable goods on the backs of donkeys. These people were the ancestors of the modern Bedouin as well as of the Jews, and it is unlikely that when the Israelites, in the persons of Joseph's brethren, first came to Egypt the Egyptian frontier guards were able to distinguish them from any other of the numerous wandering desert herds-men such as the Amorites, whose movement across the border they were paid to control. On p. 32 is a picture, as seen by an Egyptian artist, of a typical family of Amorite smiths or tinkers, with their kit of tools carried on an ass.

The Israelites probably entered Egypt early in the rule of the Hyksos or 'foreign kings' of Egypt, and indeed perhaps under their protection, since all that is known of the Hyksos is that they were not Egyptians. We do know, however, that in the

Nineteenth-century Cairo; Riding-asses with women's saddles.
[*From E. W. Lane, "Manners and Customs of the Modern Egyptians"* (1836)

century and a half during which they ruled Egypt the horse as
the motive power of battle chariots came into general use in
the Egyptian army, and that at the end of that time the Hyksos
were overthrown by a revolt of army officers, and that the
mutineers restored to the throne of Upper and Lower Egypt a
prince of native stock—presumably the Pharaoh who "knew not
Joseph".

Now from being the equals of the former rulers the Hebrews
had become a population of slaves and bondmen, so that they
did not own one horse between the lot of them, but they had
plenty of donkeys. It was on donkeys that they packed up their
few chattels and set out for the Red Sea under the leadership
of Moses on their forty-year trek, most of it through desert
country. Donkeys carried the Ark of the Covenant and the
complete portable Tabernacle of Jehovah across Sinai and
through the Negev, round the east bank of Jordan on the long,
circuitous route to Palestine. Quite early in the long march
Moses brought down from the peak of Mount Sinai the code of
Laws in ten sections which were specially framed to regulate
the life of a people perpetually on the move, and of these commandments the one about covetousness is significant. Not to be
coveted were the neighbour's ox, and his ass; and that is all the
livestock specifically mentioned, presumably to stand for the two
most valuable kinds. There were no horses and no camels. In
their present situation, of course, the cattle would have been a
liability rather than an asset to the wandering Hebrews, being
big water-drinkers, and ever hungry for the green herbage that
was not to be had along the trail. Skinny and poor these oxen
must have been, so that many were needed to move whatever
carts their owners possessed, the cows yielding barely enough
milk to feed their own calves when alive, and when dead fit
to make little but soup. But once the Hebrews got to the
Promised Land and could start farming again they would need
oxen for the plough, and so perhaps they took with them the
nucleus of a breeding herd of an African strain which they
knew would be superior to any Asiatic cattle they might in due
course be able to pick up on the far side of Wadi el Arish. But
the ass—that stood them in good stead first, last, and all the
time. Moses, quite apart from his religious leadership, acquired
a great reputation as a desert navigator and a water-diviner,

which spread among the other tribes whose paths crossed that of the Israelite column in the dry wilderness, and is still legendary today among the Bedouin. Among their countless anecdotes of Nebi Musa (the Prophet Moses) is one recounted by T. E. Lawrence.

One day, when the Children of Israel were down to their last skinful of water, and even Moses with his wonderful sixth sense for detecting water-holes was at a loss, they saw a cloud of dust on the horizon, which by the speed at which it shifted came, they knew, from a herd of wild asses on the move. Moses gave the order to change direction and follow the dust-cloud, and sure enough in due course it led them to the watering-place of the asses, a great rock from which a spring gushed. There is nothing inherently improbable in the story, whether the herd was of truly wild asses (onagers) or of escaped domestic donkeys run wild. However, it explains why certain desert tribes, full of admiration for an animal that was so superbly able to survive in the kind of country that they too were forced to inhabit as best they could, took the ass as their totem, and formed a cult in which the god took the form of a donkey, as tribal ancestor and symbol of the continuing life of the community. We shall come to some religious ideas later on in this book, but there is

Prehistoric rock-painting from Fezzan, Algeria, of herdsman wearing ritual wild-ass headdress

[*After B. Brentjes*

no doubt that a certain section of the Israelites once went in
for this donkey-cult too (just as many of them had taken up the
Egyptian cult of the bull Apis and worshipped a golden calf).
The story was hushed up as discreditable by the true believers,
but it helps to explain why the enemies of the Jews many years
later, in the time of the Romans, were able to describe them as
donkey-worshippers, and to fix this smear, by an easy association, on the Christians who shared a large part of the Jewish
tradition. The story was given wide currency in the propaganda of one Apion, called 'the Egyptian' (he was actually a
Greek, born in Libya). A don at the university of Alexandria
during the reign of the emperor Caligula, he published many
anti-Jewish writings, in which he asserted among other things
that the Jews worshipped an ass. As it happens, all his writings
are lost, and we should never have known what he said on this
subject but for the fact that the romanized Jewish historian
Josephus quoted him in the work which he wrote specially to
refute Apion. But not before an equally famous Roman historian
had read and believed the original story. Tacitus in his *History*
says: "The Jews are the descendants of Egyptian lepers and
worship an ass". Neither remark is true, but one can see how
both came about. Lepers in the ancient East were outcasts,
literally 'driven out' of the community; of course the Jews had
been driven out of Egypt. Furthermore, as we have seen, this
very period, the beginning of the Exodus, was the one in which
the donkey was of the greatest importance to the Jews, and
probably the Egyptians of that day had looked on the Israelites
as 'donkey people'—neither native ox-driving peasants nor
horse-owning aristocrats (Hyksos) but an intrusive donkey-
borne middle class. By the time of Josephus, however, the
'special relationship' had long been a thing of the past, and he
himself says of the ass, in his essay 'Against Apion', that 'the ass
is to us as to other nations—a useful beast of burden, no more
and no less'.

Perhaps the Jews learned only one point of assmanship from
the Egyptians all the time they were living beside the Nile.
There is a peculiar type of litter seen only in Egyptian pictures,
in which a pair of asses go, not tandem, but side by side. They
wear pads connected by rods, and to these is fixed a chair, in
which the passenger sits between the asses; such an equipage is

never seen borne by any other animals but asses. (Mr Robin Borwick points out that the gait of the ass is peculiarly suited to such work.) It seems the Jews adopted this Egyptian (or more likely Libyan) invention, and this is probably what is meant by the story in the Book of Judges about the Levite going to Gibeah to fetch his handmaid 'with *two* asses saddled', and being so horribly treated by the Benjamites of that town as to provoke a civil war.

The echo of the donkey-worshipping story in the early days of the Christians in Rome has only reached us in a muffled and confused form. There is more than one crude sketch daubed on a wall (one is in the Catacombs near old Christian tombs) in the style which we associate still with the lowest forms of political propaganda. It shows a crucified figure with an ass's head. This could mean either 'The Crucified One was an ass', or it could mean 'Death to the Christians!' since to the Romans the cross was simply a gallows, and there is other, verbal, evidence that donkey-worship was ascribed to Christians. Then again it could equally well be yet another anti-Jewish pictorial slogan, meaning simply 'Hang the Jews!'

However that may be, it was not the Christians, nor yet the Jews, who introduced the ass to the Roman world, or rather to Roman Europe.

3 The Donkeys Come to Europe

ALTHOUGH the ass has not achieved quite such world-wide distribution as the horse (because it cannot stand cold and humidity to the same degree as can its larger cousin), one of the most striking facts about its history is its acclimatization in China, specifically in North China, from a very early date. How did this come to pass, so very far from the ancestral home of the original wild ass? It would have to pass through territories thickly populated by other animals which are and have been used for the same tasks as those at which the ass has earned its keep for thousands of years, and which one would think were better equipped to live in the climate and on the soils of this vast space of Central Asia.

Tattoo (Ibex, tiger, ass) on right arm of mummified frozen corpse, buried *c.* 430 B.C. at Pazyryk, Western Siberia. Though the style is fantastic, the long ears must indicate a domestic donkey, not the native wild ass of the region

We have seen above in Chapter 1 that there are large tracts of Central Asia which in terms of natural history are wild-ass territory, while adjoining these lands of the onager there are others more arid still where the camel first originated, where perhaps it was first domesticated, and in which it is still used for caravan purposes. There are parts more favoured by nature where the wild horse, the Asiatic taki, once roamed in vast numbers, where it too was first domesticated, and from which the wild form has now been driven by the advance of stock-breeding nomads with their greedy, thirsty flocks and herds of sheep and goats, into the desiccated salt-caked wastes of the Gobi.

Through all these lands and many others adjacent there wound its way from time immemorial a trade route known eventually as the Silk Road: a road more than six thousand miles long, from the Pacific coasts of China to its western terminus at Alexandria, in Egypt. From very ancient times the Silk Road had a branch leading north-eastward into Siberia, along which gold was brought to the commercial centres of the Near East and the Mediterranean from the richest and most easily workable deposits of this precious metal ever known. The silk trade, and probably before it the traffic in gold from east to west, was channelled for thousands of years along this road which skirted the northern edge of the great mountain massif of the Himalayas to reach such famous markets as Tashkent and Bokhara and Samarkand. The merchants and their caravans were literally years on the way, and it seems unlikely that more than a handful of them ever made the journey in its entirety. There was a great deal of what is called entrepôt trading on the way, and each time the slim bales of yellow raw silk changed hands their prices went up and up and up. It probably rose much more steeply than the price of gold in the same caravans, being so much more bulky and liable to damage in handling and from weather. Now, each sector of the route, according to the type of country traversed, had its own characteristic draught and pack animals. In China itself in early times goods were carried in ox-carts (in the south drawn by water-buffaloes rather than oxen), but animal transport has always been scarce in China relative to the number of people, and many of the goods were probably carried by coolies or porters. Over the mountainous

stretches to the north of Tibet yaks were used, and on the grassy
plains of Mongolia, pack-horses. One would think that the wild
asses of central Asia, the kiang and the kulan, would be ideal
for this traffic, but we have no account at any period of attempts
to tame them, even though it can be shown that the Persian
Wild Ass was used in draught in early times. There is no doubt
that over the greater part of the journey camels bore the burden, but there are drawbacks about the camel as a draught
animal. For one thing, horses have an inborn antipathy to
camels unless deliberately brought into contact with them day
by day, while the camel is difficult to house owing to its stature.
Moreover, while it might not need protection from the weather,
there was the question of security. The merchant liked if possible to spend the night within four walls, with a watchman on
duty to guard him as he slept. He also liked to have his animals
as well as his cargo within those same four walls; and where
the local design of caravanserai had doors too low for a camel
to enter he would be forced to load his merchandise on some
animal that was almost as undemanding as the camel in the
matter of drink, but lower on the leg. This points to the donkey
or the mule. Now, as the businessmen sat chattering after their
supper in these wayside inns, or after the big deals in precious
metals and textiles in the markets of Turkestan, the commercial
mind would turn to the possibilities of useful minor transactions
'on the side', and there would be buying and sale of personal
effects and transport animals. There must also have been many
animals lamed by the wayside, and just able to make it as far
as the nearest rest-house. In many such cases there would be
no permanent damage—all that would be needed was rest,
which the packman on his way could not provide. His only
course was to redistribute the loads and to sell the temporarily
unroadworthy animal to the innkeeper, who would rest it and
provide such veterinary care as was current at that time and in
those parts. When it was sound again he would sell it—probably at a handsome profit, because he was negotiating from a
position of strength—to some merchant in desperate need of a
fresh load-carrier. All the animals used along the Silk Road
were more or less specialized for particular types of country,
but the ass and the mule, even more than the horse, were the
most generally useful, as able to cope more or less with all types

of country encountered. Although they were more vulnerable to cold than either the yak or the Bactrian camel—with its thick winter coat of what virtually amounts to felt—something could be done about that by rugging them up.

Here it may be appropriate to remark that most asses east of the Euphrates must have an infinitesimal amount of onager or kiang or kulan blood in their ancestry. Unlike the cross between the ass and the horse, that between the domestic African and the Asiatic wild ass is fertile, and we have a few examples, in the form of pictures on Egyptian frescoes, of hybrids—not exactly mules—which are a product of the ass-onager cross. Moreover, in Asia Minor, in Persia, and in Mesopotamia there will have been a brief period (brief by the standards of this long story, perhaps not more than a few centuries) during which the African ass and the onager were both in use, the one for pack-traffic and the other for driving. These would be crossed, either deliberately or now and again by accident, and the resultant half-breeds put to work with the other donkeys, so that by the time the pure-bred onager ceased to be used in harness—because it was displaced by the horse in the second millennium B.C.—amid the donkey-stock of Asia east of, roughly, the Orontes river there would be a thin trickle of onager blood in the veins.

Farther east along this same route, the Silk Road, the way led through the lands of the untamed kulan and kiang, larger and more weather-resistant than the Persian or Indian wild ass, and here the mixed matings would be of a very different order. It is a matter of frequent record, vouched for by eye-witnesses among the herdsmen of Mongolia, that there has been a constant exchange of blood between the taki, the almost extinct wild horse of the Mongolian steppe, and the only slightly less wild ponies of the herdsmen. But these matings are all one way. Either a mare in season breaks away from the 'tame' herd and makes off into the desert, there to be covered by a wild stallion and subsequently to be recaptured carrying a half-bred foal or having it at foot, or else some wandering taki colt, who has been driven out by the master-stallion of the wild herd (probably his own father) covers a tame mare who is hobbled and never gets away from human bondage, even for a brief honeymoon. Thus the Mongolian tame-horse stock is riddled with wild blood, some of it of fairly recent origin. But the converse never happens—that is, the progeny of the wild mare and the tame stallion hardly exists. Stallions, of course, do occasionally escape from their owners and run off into the steppe, but if they are imprudent enough to approach the wild herd they never survive their first encounter with the taki stallion, who may be much smaller and a little slower than the herdsman's horse, but who is a savage fighter and invariably leaves his domestic rival for dead.

What is true of the equine life of Central Asia must also be true of its asinine life; so that though there is a strain of the Asiatic wild ass in the tame Asiatic donkey, there is no taint of domestic blood in such herds of wild asses as survive in Asia.

When, therefore, the first working donkeys reached North China by way of the Silk Road they may well have included individuals that were no longer of unmixed descent from the Nubian Wild Ass but had an infusion of onager or kulan or kiang blood. But by that time the donkeys had also come to Europe, and we have one striking early European picture that suggests that in this case too there had been some blending of originally quite separate wild varieties. A beautifully figured Attic vase of the early fifth century B.C., now in the Museum of Fine Arts, Boston, shows a pack-ass in which all the details of saddle and harness and load are clearly drawn; equally clearly drawn are 'zebra marks' on all four legs below knee and hock, also on these joints. They are quite unmistakeable, and strongly recall to the English eye similar markings found on dun-coloured ponies of our native breeds, principally the Highland and the Connemara. They are very seldom found today on the European donkey, never on the Nubian Wild Ass, but they are a characteristic feature of the Somali Wild Ass, and the only possible conclusion can be that the first donkeys brought into Greece must have included specimens whose ancestors (or some of them) came not from Libya but from the Horn of Africa.

This seems equally probable when we consider by what means the ass reached Greece. If Greece was the portal by which it entered Europe, and in the process of centuries fanned out all over this continent, Asia Minor was the corridor down which it approached that portal, having come up through Syria and Palestine. King Solomon's South Arabian contemporary, the Queen of Sheba, traded with Africa south of the Horn (the biblical Land of Punt), and the ships of that time could carry donkeys; indeed, they could carry horses and mules too, for we learn that the first horses in the famous Stables of Solomon were imported from Asia Minor by way of Tyre. Once landed in South Arabia the distance by land to, say, Jerusalem from Aden is no greater than that from Tripoli in Libya to Jerusalem. And what is distance by land to the ass? Given not too cold a climate, and a little more time than the horse needs, no road is too long or too rough for him.

In other respects the introduction to Greece of the ass—and almost immediately of the mule also—fits in very well with a date about the lifetime of King Solomon, about the end of the first millennium B.C. The ass is linked, in Greek mythology, with the cult of the Syrian wine-god Dionysus, which spread by way of Asia Minor, Cyprus, and Crete through the Aegean Isles and eventually to the mainland of Hellas. There is a dark side to the legend of Bacchus, or Dionysus—he was, after all, the god

Local pattern of ass pack-saddle from Cyprus, one of the stepping-stones between Asia Minor and the Greek mainland
[*Photo C. Chenevix Trench*

Greek mainland pattern of pack-saddle, near Corinth, 1967
[*Photo Mary Aiken Littauer*

Same pattern of saddle on mule near Epidauros, 1967
[*Photo M. A. Littauer*

of tragedy—but there is also a more benign side, amply represented in ancient art, which shows him in a blissful state of
vinosity, tipsily perched on a steadily pacing ass. And it was in
this posture that the ass came over the horizon of the ancient
Greeks, a figure in a charade spelling out the introduction of an
important element of culture into what was still largely a
barbarous continent. For Dionysus (Bacchus) was not simply
the patron of boozers. He was the god of vine-growers and
wine-makers. Any barbarian can drink wine—it takes a civi-
lized man to tend the vine and press the grape. The reason why
Bacchus and his Etruscan counterpart Fufruns, likewise a wine-
god in Northern Italy, are shown in company with an ass is
that the ass is an essential partner in the cultivation of the vine.

It is relatively slight of build, and can be more conveniently
used than the bulky ox to till the narrow spaces between the
vines, it is sure-footed on the narrow terraces where vines were
grown on steep Mediterranean hillsides, it works more steadily
than the horse, and puts down its small feet more carefully on
a narrower track. For the same reason, it was also the ideal
beast of burden to carry the panniers of grapes in the season of
vintage, and it could be used to turn the lever of the wine-press.

Still in the field of mythology, a creature amply represented
in Greek art is the onocentaur. What, you may ask, is an onocentaur? Well, in every field the motto of the ass in regard to
the horse is 'Anything you can do, I can do too'. From the
moment of the first confrontation of the chariot-driving Greeks
with men riding horses, somewhere on the borders of Thessaly
and Thrace, the legend of the centaur—the horse with a human
torso growing out of its withers—was born, to flourish long after
riding became a commonplace activity in Greece. It was natural
and logical enough, then, for the onocentaur—the ass with
human upperworks—to be added to the menagerie of gryphons
and gorgons and the rest with which the world of Greek myth
swarmed, and be duly depicted on more than one painted vase
that survives to the present day. There were, regrettably, no
mulocentaurs. One supposes the three-way cross of ass-man-
horse was just too much for the Hellenic imagination. After all,
moderation in all things. . . .

In real life the ass was introduced along with, and as an
essential partner in, viticulture, to all the colonies which the

Greek maritime powers planted along the north shore of the
Mediterranean, as far as Spain, and including such coastal
settlements in France as Marseilles. Magna Graecia—Greater
Greece—comprised large parts of the toe-and-heel of Italy.
There too the ass followed the vine-dressing Greek colonists,
while it was brought to the north of the peninsula by the Etrus-
cans, perhaps direct from Asia Minor.

Thus the Romans at the moment when their city was founded
on the Seven Hills beside the Tiber had as their most powerful
neighbours on both hands people who possessed not only horses
but asses and, by implication, mules also. The Romans not only
made good use of the ass but helped to spread it over a wider
territory than ever before. For all their skill in government,
for all their military valour, their genius for organization, their
respect for law and order, the civilization which the Romans
spread over a great part of Europe and Africa and Asia had

Onocentaur on Greek figured vase
[British Museum

great gaps in the material, technical sense, and these gaps often yawned in a space where the Roman construction was solid up to the very brink. For instance, no people before them, and few since, have designed and built such road systems, or organized such efficient messenger services over them. Yet the load capacity of even the largest Roman vehicle was never more than half a ton, no matter how many animals were harnessed to it. The history of goods transport in Roman times—that is, for a good six hundred years—is one long, unsuccessful, and rather half-hearted attempt to solve an insoluble problem. This problem was how to adapt the double yoke, first designed for a pair of plough oxen and later attached to a wagon-pole instead of the plough-beam, to the shoulders of the horse. In fact it could not and cannot be done without great loss of mechanical efficiency, owing to the basic difference between bovine and equine anatomy, and between the head (hence neck) carriage of the horse and that of the ox. But the withers of the ass, and

The ass-riding Dionysus, painted on a Greek wine-cup
[*British Museum*

to some extent those of the mule, are less unlike those of the ox than are those of the horse, and the neck of the ass, like that of the ox, is carried horizontally. It was therefore possible, by the use of a modified yoke which was more like an inverted V fitting over the base of the neck, to produce a form of draught harness which, though it had no traces, produced fairly good results when fitted on the ass or mule. The great historian of draught harness, C. Lefebvre des Noettes, remarked that of all the conveyances known to antiquity the type of Roman wagon designed to be drawn by a team of four donkeys abreast approached nearest to modern standards of efficiency, in terms of the ratio of load carried to the combined weight of the team.

The ass, then, travelled the length and breadth of the Roman Empire, to the furthest limits to which it expanded, but not always in the same capacity: sometimes in harness, but much more often under the pack-saddle, in trade, in husbandry, and

Dionysus, mule-borne, on Greek figured vase

[*British Museum*

in military employ. To break
out of the Italian peninsula
by land the Roman armies
had first to cross the Alpine
passes, and this they could
only do if supported by a
pack-train which principally
consisted of donkeys. The
same applied to the mer-
chants (often of Syrian
birth) who followed the
armies once pacification had
taken place. As part of the
task of colonization the
Romans taught the be-
nighted provincials the
art and mystery of the vintner's craft, and pushed the
culture of the vine almost
as far north as geographical
limits of climate allow, that
is, for practical purposes, to
the latitude of the Loire. In
this capacity Roman Gaul

Corinthian clay model, *c.* 380 B.C.,
of monkey riding ass
[*British Museum*

was populated with asses, as were the provinces of Upper and
Lower Germania as far as Bonn. On the outskirts of that town
lies the most northerly vineyard in continental Europe. I have
walked through it, and drunk its excellent *Spätlese*. Further
than that, the ass was probably not bred in the Rhineland, but
it *worked* far beyond those limits. Every cohort of every Roman
legion had on its establishment a civilian sutler (*caupa*) who
marched at the rear of the column protected by a strong rear-
guard, leading a donkey on either side of whose pack-saddle
was slung a skinful of the Roman equivalent of *pinard*. Such
sutlers crossed over to the isle of Britain with the expeditionary
forces, donkeys and wine and all.

Now, while a man who has enough land for the smallest
vineyard has by implication enough grazing to support a breeding jenny, the same is not the case with an itinerant grog-shop
keeper. Therefore the ass was probably not bred in Roman

Britain, though the Roman Naafi dispensed its utility brand of
Falernian, ass-transported, right up the frontier with savage
Caledonia, as the bones of a canteen-wallah's ass found among
the ruins of the Roman fort at Newstead, in Roxburghshire,
have proved.

As long as the Empire persisted in working order, it would be
just as practical to import what asses were needed from Gaul.
But after all, it did not last for ever. There came a day when
the sun set on the Empire of the Caesars, as it has done on other
empires before and since. In that twilight of the ancient world,
when the legions had departed from Britain, there remained
throughout the southern parts of the province pockets that
were not rifled either by Saxon or by Pictish war-bands, or by
the even more dreaded Scottish pirates from across the Irish
Sea. Here where the last of the Romano-British gentry still led
something that was recognizable as Roman life, there is some
evidence that, in the face of the almost total collapse of sea-
borne trade with the Continent, attempts were made in places
with a specially favourable climate to grow vines and make
wine. They need not have been failures. Some English monasteries made their own (grape) wine in the Middle Ages, and
there are viable vineyards in Hampshire to this day. The logical
conclusion would be that to work these marginal vineyards it
would be necessary to keep asses, and to breed them also, since
imports of all kinds were becoming a thing of the past. What is
not economic in days of prosperity may become desirable and
necessary under crisis conditions, and it may well be that the
first British-bred asses were born on those run-down villas in
the first century of the Dark Ages.

East of the Rhine and north of the Danube the ass and the
mule made no progress as long as these rivers remained the
frontiers of the Roman Empire, and little thereafter, for a
variety of reasons that had nothing to do with military or political frontiers. But before turning in this direction we must see
how the ass came to press on into the most westerly (barring
Iceland) country of Europe, where it came to be regarded in
due course as a traditional feature of life—into Ireland.

Hibernia was never conquered or even reconnoitred by the
Romans. They had no economic motive for doing so, and by the
time it would have been militarily desirable to mop up the nests

áꞇoꝺꞇ ꞽoꝛꞇꝑ ꞽnꞇo phaꞽ�997onꞇ . ꝺꞽcꝛꞽꝝꞺ ꞇohꞽꞽꞽ ꞽꞽꞽꞽꝛꝛꝺꞇꞱꞽꞽꞽꞽꞽꞽꞇ
ꞇꝛꞽoꝛꝛꞽꞹ ꞹꞽꞇꞽoꝛꝛꞽ ꞽꞹꞽꝛꝑ hꞇoꝛꝛꝺꞹ ꞽꞹꞽꞇoꝛꞽ9 hꝛꝝꝝꝛꞽꝛ hꞇoꝛꝛꝺꞹ . ꞽꞇꞽꞹꞽꞽꞇꞽꞽꞹ

Reasonably realistic Anglo-Saxon miniature painting of asses
[British Museum

of pirates which descended from its shores, to plague the shipping of the later Empire, such an enterprise was beyond
the capabilities of any Roman commander in the West. There
were no asses in Dark Age Ireland, none in medieval Ireland,
none in the Ireland over which the Tudors claimed, and partly
exercised, sovereignty.

Among all the wealth of illustrations to Thomas Derrick's
Image of Ireland (1581) there is nary an ass at all. Indeed,
at this time the asinine penetration of Devon and Cornwall was
only making headway very slowly, and expansion into the other
island must have begun some time between then and the Crom-
wellian Plantation, at first on quite a modest scale. Just as the
Roman ass first came to Britain behind the Imperial eagles, so
the English armies brought the ass to Ireland: not in the official
wagon train, but somewhere in the scandalous caravan of
sutlers and strumpets and grog-shop keepers that followed
every army in the seventeenth century, including the pious
Presbyterian Parliamentary hosts; psalm-singers in the van,
bawlers of bawdy ballads bringing up the rear.

Throughout the eighteenth century Ireland, as a source of
cheap remounts, was denuded of horses in the course of the
many wars with France, culminating in the twenty-year conflict
with Napoleon. During these wars the British losses in cavalry
horses were very heavy (how many troop horses were shot on
Vigo beach alone, because there was no room for them in the

crowded transports which had come to take off Sir John Moore's force?). India also swallowed up a lot of horseflesh, until the sensible solution was arrived at of buying the cheaper sort of Arabs—which stood the climate so much better—from the Gulf traders. But as the Irish countryside began to be swept clean of horses that could be bought for under £10, the gap came to be filled by donkeys. The kind of small farmer with whom the remount-purchasers concluded their rather one-sided deals was probably much better pleased with his price than an English farmer would have been, and, seeing all that cash in one lump, would be reluctant to reinvest it all at once; instead he could buy with it a couple of asses, and still have enough left over for 'contingencies'.

This drain of horseflesh, the vacuum being filled up by donkeys, went on in Ireland side by side with a general process that had the same effect. As the Ascendancy progressed, so the gulf widened between the anglicized classes who could afford to keep horses, and those whom the Elizabethan adventurers had called the 'mere Irish'—still hardly English-speaking—who had once had a horse, or a share in a horse, per man, but were now gradually depressed below the economic level where horse-keeping was still a possibility. The ass marched westward out of the Pale as the screw tightened upon the once-wild Irish, and saturation point and the Atlantic coast were reached at about the same time. Now the donkey is to be seen as frequently in Galway as in any other part of the country, but the Gaeltacht of Connemara is probably the last corner of Ireland into which it expanded, and there it has existed side by side with the Connemara pony. For Connemara, the last refuge alike of the Irish language and the horse-owning, horse-breeding peasant, is having a comeback as a source of very superior ponies which are being sold across the Irish Sea and the Atlantic at prices that would have flabbergasted the dealers, not of the last generation but of twenty or even twelve years ago. Is something of the sort about to befall the Irish ass also?

Life was really only supportable for the Irish ass because of the relatively mild climate, where the absence of really savage and prolonged winter cold does something to compensate for a climate that is really too humid for the animal to maintain its full stature. It is, after all, the product of a drier environment than the horse. It made much less, and much slower, progress on the continent of Europe between the same degrees of latitude as those of Ireland, primarily because of the cold winters, but also, perhaps, because the greater part of Central and Eastern Europe in the 50 to 55 degrees North range was—and largely still is—heavily wooded, and the ass wild or tame is not really a forest-dwelling species. Thus it never reached Scandinavia in significant numbers at all. France demonstrates very clearly the climatic limitations of the ass. It is still fairly common in the south, but it has always been comparatively rare in the north.

As we have seen, the ass was established in the Rhineland in Roman times, but only became known east of that river during the Middle Ages. Its advance towards the Baltic was slow and spasmodic, and undertaken in partnership with one of its oldest allies—the Jewish dealer. Just as Joseph's brethren had loaded their corn sacks on to asses to go to fill them in Egypt thousands of years earlier, so Jewish merchants who had been established in the Rhineland since long before the days of Charlemagne followed the expansion of German rule into Central Europe. Some of them were in a very small way of business—mere pedlars—and a donkey-sized pack was the very thing to contain their stock-in-trade of buttons and bobbins, brushes and combs. Others handled goods of high intrinsic value, or were craftsmen in precious metals. For such men an unpretentious appearance was the safest form of insurance.

In times and places where a horse meant prestige, a horse was to be avoided. Hence the pedlar's moke and the goldsmith's moke, which, it seems, arrived simultaneously on the European borders of Russia with that dialect of medieval German known as Yiddish.

The farther one moves away from the Mediterranean, the less realistic become the efforts of medieval artists to depict the donkey as an unavoidable illustration to certain biblical scenes. Some artists in Norway and Iceland gave up the struggle altogether. There are early altar-cloths in the latter country with scenes from the Flight into Egypt which portray the Virgin and Child on what does not pretend to be anything else but an Icelandic pony. Understandably, since the artist had never seen a live ass.

By contrast with this sort of thing, the pictures of donkeys in early English bibles are comparatively true to life, and taken together with the lack of difficulty which the Anglo-Saxon writers had in translating passages from Latin works where the animal is mentioned, the presence among early English place-names of some which probably mean 'donkey-farm' (and still more which, as will be seen in the next chapter, can be construed as 'mule-farm') and the existence of an Old English nickname which presumably means 'ass'[1] all lead one to suppose that the ass was not such a rarity in Britain in Anglo-Saxon times as one might think.

There is mention of a stud jackass at Burton-on-Trent in the twelfth century, but in general the donkey in early medieval England was confined to the drier eastern side of the country, and did not spread to Devon and Cornwall until the days of Elizabeth I. Richard Carew of Antony, whose *Survey of Cornwall* was written in the last years of that reign, says that "not long since one brought over a he-ass from France *because of the strangeness of the beast*, who following his kind begat many monsters, viz. Mules, and for monsters indeed the country people admired them; yea, some were so wise as to knock on the head or give away the issue of his race, as uncouth mongrels". Which says enough for the unfamiliarity of the Cornishman of that day with the asinine race. But Carew also points to the reason why the donkey finally 'took on' in Cornwall and West Devon, "since the statute 12th of King Henry viiith", which empowered sheriffs to confiscate sub-standard ponies found grazing on commons. In the greater part of England some four-fifths of all ponies will have been sub-standard, because the

[1] *Esla.*

Sussex asses in harness and at grass

[*Bayeux Tapestry*

only specification laid down was one of height. Most of the time the local authorities did not enforce this law at all strictly, and many classes (*e.g.*, men with common rights on Exmoor and the New Forest) were exempt from it. But for some reason it was rigorously applied in the far West. No such regulations were enacted about donkeys and mules, and Carew himself advised smallholders and "ordinary husbandmen . . . to quit breeding of horses and be-

Jacobean Londoner with washing and donkey, 1625
[*British Museum*

take themselves to mules, for that is a beast that will fare hardly, live very long, and . . ." but that would draw us into the matter of the following chapter. Suffice it to say here that the trend towards donkeys in 'Wessex' was accelerated from that time onward, not so much because Carew's advice was followed, but because the very extensive commons began to be enclosed, leaving only perilous strips along the cliff-tops, such as survive even now between Hartland and Bude. A horse on these stands a constant risk of going over the edge, especially if chased. But a donkey has more common sense, and a better footing on steep slopes.

Apart from Carew's informant and his like, rich enough to bring over a he-ass from France (doubtless a Poitou giant), the donkey was probably brought into Devon and Cornwall by the gipsies who had for long been keeping it on the dry heaths of Norfolk. Certainly when the Romanies first arrived in the New Forest they had not two horses to rub together, and all the earliest English pictures of gipsies show them carrying all their goods on pack-asses, without wagons, and living entirely in benders.

4 *Without Pride of Ancestry or Hope of Posterity*

> Now these are the generations of Esau, who is Edom. Esau took his wives of the daughters of Canaan: Adar, the daughter of Elon the Hittite, and Aholibamah the daughter of Anah the son of Zibeon the Hivite.
>
> *Genesis* xxxvi, 1, 2
>
> AND these are the children of Zibeon; both Ajah, and Anah; this was that Anah that found the mules in the wilderness, as he fed the asses of Zibeon his father.
>
> *Ibid.*, v. 24

THE Jews were forbidden by their religion to breed mules, because the coupling of animals of different species was held to be contrary to the laws of Nature, and hence to the commandments of God. It is typical of the scrupulous literal-

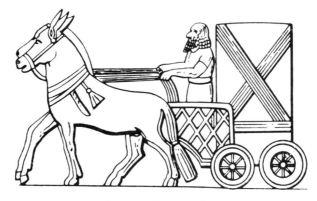

Assyrian mule-team drawing heavy wagon
[*After H. Potratz*

mindedness of the Hebrew legal system that this taboo was held to apply also to the yoking of different animals together at work, and no man among the Jews might plough with an ox and an ass, an ass and a horse, a horse and a camel, under the one yoke. But it is also typical of a certain kind of double-think, not peculiar either to the Israelites or to antiquity, that the Jews did not therefore refrain from buying and using the mule resulting from this forbidden union—in fact, they were great patrons of mule-breeding carried on by neighbouring peoples, and took great pride at times in good mule-powered turn-outs. Such an attitude of mind is to be seen in medieval Christians, who deemed it impious to lend money at interest, but saw no harm in borrowing it at interest, and thus creating a demand which the Jews above all were willing and able to satisfy. This demand having being satisfied, the borrowers of yesterday were quite happy to turn round and demand the punishment of the wicked usurers.

Among the chief suppliers of mules to the Israelite market

Clay model of two-mule cart, Corinth, 350 B.C.

we might mention Hittites. In their script is preserved not only the first known manual on training the racehorse, but also some very early price regulations, including a schedule of approved prices for livestock, in which the standard price of a horse is 20 sheep,[1] of an ox 10 sheep, and of a mule 60 sheep. The mule is so expensive because of its triple utility. It can be used for pack transport, like the donkey, for ploughing and heavy draught, like the ox, and for riding, like the horse. As a riding-animal it had a great advantage due to its mixed parentage. There is a phenomenon known as hybrid vigour, which in certain cases results in the progeny of an extreme outcross (and you cannot have a more pronounced outcross than the mating of two separate species), being larger and stronger than either parent.

[1] 1 sheep = 1 shekel.

Moorish kettle-drummer
riding mule
[*Drawn by Rembrandt.*
British Museum

In the case of the hinny or jennet (foal of donkey mare by horse) this does not operate, but the mule proper (foal of mare by jackass) is often taller than either parent. In the world of the Hittites, where the only available domestic horse was seldom taller than the thirteen-hand wild tarpan from which it was descended, a mule that might grow to over fourteen hands was potentially a very valuable property. Ridden by a general, for instance, it would give him a wider field of view over the battle-ground, and ridden by his standard-bearer it would render the standard so much more conspicuous.

It is precisely in this role that we see the mule being used in Oriental armies over a long period; also as the mount of trumpeters and drummers. These transmitted the commander's orders by prearranged blasts on the trumpet or (especially in the case of the Turks) rolls on the kettledrum, and in order that the commander should be able to find and keep in touch with them too they were mounted on the tallest and most conspicuous animals: if these could be odd-coloured, so as to stand out from the crowd, so much the better.

The mule must necessarily appear first at a comparatively late date in the history of the ass (if the reader will pardon a blinding glimpse of the obvious), since mules cannot be produced unless domestic horses are available. Specifically, brood-mares are needed to produce mules proper. It is just possible that jennets could be born to the tame she-ass, as a result of the attentions of a wandering wild or runaway stallion. But the wild horse never existed south of the highlands which separate the Fertile Crescent from the basins of those rivers which run into the Caspian and the Black Sea; and the spread of tame horses southward across the same barrier was slow by comparison with their expansion into Persia and India and westward along the northern and southern shores of the Black Sea from the Oxus region. In biblical terms, it is unlikely that mules could have been bred in the Syrian/Palestine/Jordan region much before the time of Joseph, since the earliest remains of a horse that had certainly been in human care so far discovered is the skeleton of a solitary gelding, buried about 1750 B.C. with military honours, inside the Egyptian fort of Buhen, on the frontier of Nubia. Furthermore, this specimen did not appear to have worked in any capacity, it was simply an expensive and

Pair-mule cart, Boeotia, sixth century B.C. Wicker-bodied cart
with disc wheels; draught pole and yoke visible
[*Vase in British Museum*

exotic regimental mascot.

The biblical anecdote of Anah and his mules is therefore all
the more surprising, since on any showing Anah must have
lived before the time of Joseph, and a great many interesting
possibilities lie behind the brief verses which stand at the head
of this chapter. Mules in the plural are an unlikely thing to
find in the desert, since in the nature of things there is no such
thing as a family group or wild herd of mules. On the other
hand, Anah was a professional donkey-herd. If the sentence
would bear the construction 'invented' instead of 'found', then
the whole thing would make sense. (For what it is worth, the
Latin for 'found' is *invenuit*.) He would have the jackass available, and if by chance he could get hold of some mares—even
unworkably lame mares—he would have the foundations of the
first mule-stud in the world. The taboo against mating different
species was not valid for him—he was not a Hebrew but a
Hivite, the father-in-law of Esau the Edomite (Jordanian).
That is to say, he was a member of a nomadic tribe closely
related to the Hebrews, differing from them physically not at

all and linguistically very little, but in terms of religion and material culture quite considerably. Anah and his like were pagans, herdsmen and hunters, as was Esau the Hairy, rather than herdsmen and occasional cultivators like the Hebrews proper.

Anah's name is significant, being simply an old Semitic word for 'ass'. Now, such names are not uncommon in the vocabulary of Near Eastern and European peoples. Think only of a few— the respectable Hebrew Caleb, which means Dog (*cf.* Arabic *kelb*), and corresponds closely to the Gaelic MacCunn and Old Norse Hunding. Or Leo. Or the Old English Wulf and its numerous combinations. Or the Old Welsh March and Old English Hengest, both meaning Stallion. Or the Old Norse Björn—Bear. Such names are given (i) for vaguely defined traditional reasons—because they are already 'in the family'; (ii) as nicknames, mostly acquired at or near maturity, and more in the nature of surnames than first names; (iii) for religious reasons, the name of the totem animal, or the animal that personifies the god, being adopted by the family which professes that god's cult. (This is almost certainly the reason for names like Hengest and Horsa.) Now, Anah could have been so called for reason (ii) above, just as a Welsh shepherd might become known to Anglo-Welsh acquaintances as Evans the Sheep. But much more likely, as a man of the desert, he owed religious allegiance to the Set cult, or something like it, and wore his name as the Libyan herdsman pictured on p. 39 wore his donkey's-head mask, in honour of the Lord of the Wilderness.

But again, if the reason were only (i) above, we are left with the impression of the scion of an ass-breeding family, a man steeped in donkey-lore, and that is how we would imagine the first mule-breeder, rather than as a horseman and the son of a horseman. And for the purposes of mule-breeding, it is donkey-men who start with possession of the male principle, so revered throughout the intensively masculine-dominated Oriental society.

For hybrid vigour, which gave them the durable, thrifty, and *tall* mule, out of a mare by a jackass, did not work that way in the case of the jennet, sired by a stallion out of a she-ass; the jennet has other virtues, as we shall see later, but it never has the stature of the mule, owing to a rule-of-thumb which governs the breeding of equines, and runs something like this: whether in outbreeding or inbreeding, the progeny may inherit much of the conformation and some of the temperament of the sire, but they are more likely to be the height of the dam, or nearer to it than to that of the sire. In other words, to breed for size, choose the biggest females; to breed for 'make and shape', choose the handsomest males.

And here we see the perils that confront the layman using biblical sources for historical purposes. The above quotation from the Authorized Version stands side by side with equally esteemed translations, whose authors render the word that here stands for mules as 'hot springs'. One simply cannot win.

It is somewhat suspicious, however, that no further reference to mules occurs in Holy Writ down to the times of David and his sons, that is, round about the year 1000 B.C., which fits much better into the general picture, and accords with a wider distribution and use of horses in Palestine and Arabia. We have frequent mention of mules among other animals brought as tribute to the kings of Israel in the days of their expansion, and a most interesting account of a coronation ceremony—the first recorded one that bears in some ways a notable resemblance to the ceremony still in use in England. One son, Solomon—chosen according to Oriental custom out of the very numerous progeny of David, and not necessarily his eldest son, as the heir-apparent—was proclaimed king; and "all the people said: 'God save King Solomon'". But the symbol which David had chosen for the appointment of the undoubted King of Israel was the setting of Solomon on David's own personal riding-mule. Just as in Anglo-Saxon poetry the saddle is called 'the high seat of the King'.

After a period of adversity, the Captivity in Babylon, Cyrus King of the Persians repatriated 42,360 Israelites, who seem to have been once more in affluent circumstances, charging them to go home to Jerusalem and rebuild Solomon's temple. Between them the returning Israelites had 7337 slaves, 736 horses, 245 mules, 435 camels, and 6720 asses. These figures, confirmed by both Ezra and Nehemiah, probably represent pretty accurately the proportions of various kinds of transport animals available in Mesopotamia at that time. With this difference—that whereas the slave in the Israelite community was a domestic servant, in the Persian, Babylonian, Egyptian, and other Near Eastern empires the slave was just another transport animal.

The mule followed his father the ass into Europe by the same route as the latter—out of Asia Minor by way of Greece and then up the Balkan Peninsula, also by sea to Sicily, Southern Italy, and such western Greek colonies as Marseilles. This is certainly true, but in what exact sense we shall never know—that is, there is no means of telling whether the first mules came to Europe 'ready-made' or whether only the idea of breeding mule-foals instead of horse-foals from mares was imported, together with the necessary jackasses.

The Roman (ultimately Celtic) mare-goddess Epona also extended her protection to mules which, like horses, are 'the foals of mares'

What is certain is that though the early European mule was identical in type with the mule of the Levant, its function in the new continent was different. The idea of using the mule as an officer's charger never caught on in Europe. Pack-train operatives welcomed it with enthusiasm, because a good stout mule can at a pinch carry more than the 224 pounds which has been the standard European pack-horse load for the last twenty-five centuries or so. The mule was also used, in the Mediterranean lands as in Asia, for ploughing, and as a riding animal. Not, indeed, among royal families, but by ladies of rank and the ecclesiastical upper crust, both pagan and, later on, Christian. The reason for this was that many European cults, including at one time Christianity, had a taboo on the riding of horses by priests, and by means of the mule this could be very conveniently circumvented.

But the real European innovation was the use of the mule in harness, something comparatively rare in the ancient East. The classic passage is in the *Odyssey*, where the Princess Nausicaa is described by Homer as driving a mule-cart, in company with her ladies-in-waiting, with the palace laundry to a stream near the sea-shore where they were accustomed to do the washing.

Mules are mentioned more than once in the *Iliad* and the *Odyssey*, thus confirming what we might assume anyway from the evidence of Greek art, even of the early period, that they were much prized as harness animals for peaceful purposes, even though the war-chariot was exclusively drawn by horses. In the famous horse-race described in detail in the *Iliad*, one of the prizes for which the aristocratic contestants strove (it was very much a race for 'gentlemen drivers' only) was an unbroken six-year-old brood-mare, in foal to a jackass, thus showing that mule-breeding was an occupation worth the detailed attention of the upper classes, if not actually at the time of the Trojan war (say 1200 B.C., and we do not see why not) then indisputably at the time the Homeric poems were written, about 800 B.C.

How much the Homeric heroes paid for a mule we do not know, but get some idea of relative values from this prize-list. The brood-mare was offered as second prize. The third prize was a large vessel, not described in great detail, but probably one of those elaborate jereboam-sized wine-mixers decorated with reliefs round the rim, showing beautiful young men and chariot teams, of which we have so many fine examples from tombs of a somewhat later period than this. But the fourth was two talents of gold, in cash, so the vessel must have been worth more than this, and the mare worth more still. The first prize was a young and attractive female slave, accomplished at all useful domestic arts, and a trivet for her to cook on.

One more thing. The *Iliad* says of the mare (in Chapman's version), "That which *then* had high respect", as if it were no longer so in Homer's own day. Why should this be so? Perhaps because in the early days of mule-breeding, quite soon after the introduction of the ass into Europe, people had great difficulty in selecting the right kind of mare to put to a jackass: but once the right sort (what the French call *jument mulassière*) had been pin-pointed the market eased a little. Mules became more plentiful, and potential dams of mules were available. After all, there was plenty of time for this development between Diomed's day and Homer's—some four hundred years.

Greek vase paintings of the light, high-wheeled cart such as was drawn by mules even as early as this are quite common, and the pattern of cart is easily recognizable as the graceful,

The Mule of Inchbrayock: Pictish stone carving, and a Caledonian puzzle-picture of the Dark Ages. Below is Samson, recognizable by his long hair and the jawbone of an ass which he carries. Above Nimrod(?), on his mule, hunts what is evidently meant to be the wild ass; but its ears are too long.
[*National Museum of Antiquities, Scotland*

high-wheeled, gaily painted Sicilian cart, such as can be seen today, still often drawn by mules. Incidentally, this was probably one of the earliest types of European cart to be fitted with proper shafts instead of a draught-pole, the design having been modified by the Saracen invaders of Sicily, who brought the new invention (which is ultimately of Chinese origin) westward as a by-product of the Moslem conquest of such Central Asiatic territories as Samarkand. The mules of Greek and more especially of Roman times were not used for racing, but they were extensively used as teams for fast, light, *smart* civilian private carriages: and here the element of fashion entered into play, once more making the top-class mule an expensive commodity. On the military side, the Roman mule played a more prosaic part—under a pack-saddle in the supply train.

Perhaps among the descendants of the Most Northerly Roman Donkey mentioned in the last chapter may be counted the Mule of Inchbrayock. A Pictish carved monument at this place in Angus, a monument probably of the eighth century, shows what is believed to be an excerpt from the biblical story of Samson, complete with jawbone of an ass, in the lower panel of the back of a cross slab; above it is a hunting scene, the hunter being out after onager (or what the Pictish sculptor thought of as onager) and mounted on a mule, identifiable by its long ears, thin tail, and totally different appearance from the horses which are so frequently the subject of Pictish art. Certainly, if drawn from life on the spot, the model will have been in its day the Most Northerly British Mule. But at any rate, what is surprising is that anyone in Angus between 700 and 800 should have known what a mule looked like. The rider is dressed and equipped exactly like 'native' Pictish figures in similar but less exotic hunting scenes of the period, where the quarry is wolf or red deer or hare or boar.

> He fell sick suddenly, and grew so ill
> He could not sit his mule.
>
> SHAKESPEARE, *King
> Henry VIII*

A Norman vavasour, Count Guy de Ponthieu, with goshawk on fist, riding a saddle-mule considered good enough for falconry
[*Bayeux Tapestry*

The   jennet-riding
Cecil portrait from
Hatfield House
[*Ashmolean
Museum, Oxford*

So ended, at Dunstable Priory, the last journey of Cardinal
Wolsey, the last of many days spent travelling the roads of
England on the business of church or state.

And all on mule-back. This was the end of a long tradition
whereby English ecclesiastics of rank travelled, if very old or
infirm, in a mule-borne litter, but if fit rode a mule. This custom
did not outlive the Reformation by very long, but the last traces
of it are to be seen in the early 17th century, kept up by lay-
men in certain offices. There is a splendid picture at Hatfield
House of Lord Burleigh, the father of the first Robert Cecil,
riding what is more probably a jennet than a mule, and it
appears that down to the reign of James I the Lord Chancellor and certain senior law officers of the Crown were always
so mounted on official occasions.

There is no doubt that this is something that had "rubbed off"
on the lawyer and the civil servant from the days when about
half the lawyers were churchmen, practitioners of canon not
civil and criminal law; for instance, for a long while the Probate

and Divorce Courts were staffed by ecclesiastical lawyers. The distinction was more marked in England than in Mediterranean countries, where the mule was an acceptable substitute for the palfrey, ambler or "travelling horse" among the class who could afford such an animal; and, though down in the South, the Pope was never seen mounted on anything else, or bishops either. It was also quite common to see Kings of Aragon or Castile or Navarre, or Doges of Venice, for instance, mule-borne.

What seems, in England, to have distinguished the ecclesiastical lawyer from other churchmen was that the former always rode a docked mule, but this mutilation was not practised in episcopal stables.

I have not been able to discover how far down the hierarchy the use of mules descended, but it is to be noted that in the cavalcade of Chaucer's Canterbury pilgrims the Canon, most senior clergyman of the party, is riding a horse. But a little later an illustration to Lydgate's *Siege of Thebes* shows an ordinary monk riding a mule. The significant thing is that the mule was not only considered suitable for travelling with a Prince of the Church, but also for the complement to travelling, the ceremonial entry into towns and great estates along the way. Great lords such as the Percys of Northumberland kept, in addition to their travelling palfreys, special "great double-backed horses" onto which they would change at such stages, so as to make an impressive entry, gambading and cavorting and performing other airs of the High School. Their spiritual counterparts did the same thing on mule-back. There must, therefore, have been a very special class of mule capable of such airs, such as that shown on the tomb of the Cardinal du Prat, who was a contemporary of Wolsey. The Mule of State, in fact.

There is no doubt that this custom was introduced by the Normans and gained ground very slowly. Both the ass and the mule had been known in England since Roman times, but neither was especially associated by the Anglo-Saxons with the Church. Before the Conquest both priests and bishops rode horses, and indeed Bede tells us that St. Cuthbert in his ministry was commanded by the King of Bamburgh to ride a horse, which the King gave him, rather than wear out his feet on the roads of Northumberland and Durham. Wilfrid, the Yorkshire

Monk on mule with expensive trappings and elaborate curb bit. Early fifteenth-century miniature illumination from Lydgate's *Siege of Thebes.* Canterbury is in the background
[*Mansell Collection, British Museum*

nobleman turned missionary, who converted the heathen South Saxons, also travelled the length and breadth of Sussex on horseback. But this was a deliberate act of defiance and identification arising from a repudiation of heathen customs. Early English ecclesiastics rode stallions, deliberately, because the priests of many pagan cults had been forbidden by custom to do so. Again in Bede, the dramatic story of the conversion of the King of York and his High Priest, Coefi, comes to its climax when Coefi jumps onto a stallion and leads the attack on the heathen temple over whose rites he had presided for so long, deliberately breaking the taboo and thus inviting the wrath of his former master, Woden.

In Normandy, this tradition was unknown or forgotten. Great lords, both clergy and lay, often rode mules, as the picture of Count Guy de Ponthieu out hawking on his mule shows us. But bishops in Normandy, as in all the lands between there and Italy, rode mules on state occasions exclusively. As time passed, the custom took hold in the English Church, but it was still not universal in the time of Henry II, because his Chancellor and Archbishop, Thomas Beckett, rode a horse: but was the last holder of such offices to do so in England for some centuries. For one thing, in the time of the Angevin kings many western provinces of France had fallen into the domain of the English Crown; among them Poitou, which was the greatest producer of the quality mule in Western Europe, and where the tradition was carried on down to our time by the *Syndicat des Eleveurs Mulassiers des Deux-Sèvres.*

There must, I thought, be a clause of canon law which says that bishops must ride mules; alternatively, must not ride horses. I therefore asked a friend, who is a devout and well-read Catholic and a practical horseman, to find out for me when this regulation came in—whether, for instance, it was something quite new round about 1066 that had not penetrated to Britain.

My learned friend, after diligent searching of the Papal Index of Bulls, drew blank. There was literally nothing in the regulations.

So why? The answer can only be that this, like many early Church customs, is an almost unconscious takeover from Jewish practice. Among the Jews, and particularly before the time of King Solomon, the horse was looked on as something alien to Israel and regarded with deep distrust, being thought of as the mount of hostile northern nomads or the Egyptian and Babylonian oppressors. The rank-and-file of Israel rode asses, but the royal house, the Children of Jesse, rode mules. And this tradition, which carried over into early Christian practice, is vividly demonstrated in 1 Kings 1 : 38, where Solomon is chosen out of all the numerous children of David's harem as heir apparent, and the king's personal mule figures in a sort of premature coronation ceremony:

> So Zadok the priest and Nathan the prophet and Benaiah the son of Jehoiada, and the Cherethites and the Pelethites went down, and caused Solomon to ride upon King David's mule. . . .

The holder of one of the great public offices in Tudor England had to maintain much the same sort of establishment as a
senior peer of the realm like Northumberland. We can compare
the two by means of the detailed account that George Cavendish, gentleman usher to Cardinal Wolsey, gives of the transport department of Wolsey's household at the height of the
latter's fortunes, when he was at the same time Archbishop of
York and Lord Chancellor with this advantage, that Cavendish
also gives details of the personnel, as follows:

> In the stabyl he had a mayster of his horses, a clarke of the
> stabyl, a yoman of the same, a sadler, a farier, a yoman of his
> chariot, a sompter man, a yoman of his stirrope, *a mewlyter*, six-
> teen gromes of hys stabyl, every one of them kepying four grete
> geldynges.

The first three have general supervisory duties; yeoman at
this period usually means some kind of foreman. Then follow
two tradesman N.C.O.'s. The yeoman of the chariot probably
drove the same, as well as having supervision of the two grooms
who looked after the chariot horses. The sumpter man, often
called the 'lademan' in the North, would have charge of four
pack-horses according to commercial pack-train standards of
the time. The yeoman of the stirrup was not a foreman except
in the sense that he was the immediate superior of the muleteer; he was the personal attendant of the Cardinal whenever
the latter rode, and looked after his personal saddlery, which
as we shall see below was no light charge. The muleteer had a
fairly easy time, since he only had to care for two mules.
Granted the usual overstaffed conditions of the time, one groom
only to each four great horses seems a very modest ratio, but
perhaps these had their own unestablished hangers-on.

The total number of animals comprised two mules and sixty-
four great geldings. But besides these, and not kept at the town
house in Westminster, we must reckon the eight 'great stoned
trotting horses' which by statute every Archbishop was required
to maintain for breeding purposes. The chariot team would
account for eight out of the sixty-four geldings—normally six
in the traces, and two spare. The remainder were ridden by
fifty-six gentlemen of the household. But the chariot yeoman
also had a "nagge" which he rode while driving the team (there

was still no such thing as driving from the box). That makes, with the four sumpter horses, sixty-seven horses and two mules. But there were also, not mentioned here but at the end of Cavendish's account when he petitioned the King for transport to take his personal effects home after the death of his master, upward of six carts, probably with two horses each. Cavendish asked for a cart and two horses, and was given one cart and "vi of the best horses that I (could) choose amongst all my lorde's cart horses. . .".

There must have been over eighty animals in the Cardinal's stables at any one time, to maintain the requisite 'state'. Of these only the two mules were ever ridden by Wolsey himself:

> when he came to the hall door there was attendant for him his mewle, trapped altogether in crymmosyn velvet and gylt stir-

Detail of Benozzo Gozzoli's *Journey of the Magi* from the Riccardi Palace, Florence. Distinguished (Medici) ecclesiastic riding mule.
[*Mansell Collection*

ropes ... whan he was mounted with his crossbearers (2) and his pillerbearers (2) also upon grete horses trapped with red skarlett, then marched he forward with hys trayne and furniture in maner as I have declared ... and his spare mewle followynge him with lyke apparel. His sumpter mewles which were 20 in number, with his carts and other cariages of his trayne. ...

Nevertheless, for purposes of 'state'—or, to put it more crudely, ostentation—the Great Horse was not exclusively employed. The more expensive kind of jennet was also used to mount retainers, especially in France, as Cavendish himself shows us in his account of his entertainment much later on by a French lord whom he calls M. Creekey(?) at his chateau near Compiègne

where his genyt stode for him to mount upon, with xii other genettes, the most fairest beastes that ever I saw and in espaciall his owen which was a mare jennet. He shewed me that he might have had for her 400 crownes. But uppon all the other xii gennets were mounted xii goodly young gentilmen called pages of honour.

Again, at Pynkney Castle on the Somme he saw

Madam Regent the kynges mother ryding in a very rich chariot and in the same with her was her daughter the Queen of Naver, furnysshed with 100 ladyes and gentilwomen, and more folowyng, riding upon wyght palfreys; over and besides dyvers other ladyes and gentilwomen that rode some in rich chariots and some in horse litters. Then ... the Kyng came ryding uppon a goodly gennett.

Such gennetts were either Spanish or of reputed Spanish breeding. There is supporting evidence to show that in this instance Cavendish really did mean by a 'gennett' what we today mean by a jennet, and not, however spelt, some translation of the Spanish *jinete*, which was a quality pony bred in Galicia or the Asturias and trained to pace, amble, and rack. This latter meaning was the more common one among English writers of the sixteenth and seventeenth centuries, however.

In spite of these special instances, Western Europe down to about 1700 was divided into two zones according to whether there was or was not a plentiful supply of 'quality' mules and hinnies for saddle purposes. In Britain, in Northern France, in the Low Countries, Scandinavia, and Germany, people who could afford it rode, for pleasure, for hunting, and for ordinary

Hunting on a docked mule. Engraving by Stradanus (Jan van Straten) in the British Museum

[*British Museum*

travel, some kind of light horse, usually rather low on the leg and long in the back, known variously as an *ambleur* in France, a palfrey in England, a *Zelter* in Germany, or a *tjaldari* in Scandinavia. A very good stamp of palfrey was bred in Spain, and yet Spain was typical of the countries in which this function was not exclusively performed by horses. There, and in Italy, Roussillon, Provence, and Portugal, the palfrey's job was as often as not performed by a mule or a hinny. For the ass itself can be trained to amble and pace instead of trotting, and it was found possible to breed pacing mules out of pacing mares; mules which paced naturally from birth. A refinement of training was required of the mules which worked under the litter—the normal vehicle used to convey ladies over the Spanish sierras. It has been remarked that the action of a single animal when pacing is like that of two men carrying a stretcher and marching in step. But in order that the pair of mules, smoothly pacing, should impart the smoothness of their gait to the litter it was necessary that they should themselves keep step with each other. Spain was in fact one of the last European countries to adopt the coach, but when coaches became established in that country in the seventeenth century no attempt was made to breed a 'Spanish Carriage Horse'. Instead mules were used; and what fine animals they were can be seen in the Velásquez picture *Philip IV at the Boar Hunt*. They were bred out of Andalusian mares by Catalan jackasses.

The ambling palfrey, then, existed in all Mediterranean countries, but in smaller numbers than in the 'Atlantic' countries, because side by side with it the palfrey-type mule was available. This alternative 'soft ride' was carried over to the Spanish dominions in the New World without a break, and it is fair to say that the tradition of the 'easy-paced' horse and mule is more honoured in Hispanic America today than in Old Spain. Among the handful of horses of which we have a complete catalogue in the *Relacion* of Hernan Cortes—his report on his conquest of Mexico in 1519–21—we have among the preponderance of dark-coloured Andalusian war-stallions one 'pacing grey mare'—obviously a palfrey from the Biscayan provinces. Ten years later the first shipment of jackasses for breeding purposes was sent out to New Spain.

Both in the islands of the Caribbean and in various parts of Central and South America the Biscayan type of ambling palfrey is still bred and worked, shown and raced, under various names such as *caballo de paso*, *galiceño*, *paso fino*, and alongside it there still flourishes the *mulo de paso*. This is notably so in Peru, where there was from the first a demand for pack-mules because the most fertile part of the country is separated from the coast by a low-lying desert region in which the llama, the Andean beast of burden, cannot operate (in any case, the llama at best can only carry half a horse-load). But there was and is also in Peru a keen demand for a riding-mule, and the methods of Peruvian mule-breeders are of interest. Male donkey foals are selected for breeding purposes before the age of weaning, selection being based in part on their tendency to pace naturally. They are then taken off the jenny and put on a mare. It is important that they should be suckled by a mare, so that

Artillery mule carrying ammunition to the siege of Montereggio in
the Italian wars of Charles V and Francis I. Mules still carried
ammunition to the siege of Monte Cassino in 1944. Engraving by
Stradanus in the British Museum

[British Museum

they will get the impression that there is no difference between
themselves and the horse foals running in the same herd—
what animal psychologists today call 'imprinting'. There has to
be a compromise in the methods that are used to reconcile
different species to mating with each other. The donkey colt is
fostered on a mare partly also so that he shall smell horsier, and
less like an ass; but likewise before the brood mare is brought to
be covered by the adult jackass her mane is shorn to make her
look more like a jenny.

It is possible to breed the hybrid counterpart of every type
of horse. Thus in Argentina there was for many years a strong
trade in mules of the draught type, and large numbers of such
harness mules were imported by the Allies in the First World
War to serve in artillery teams. The mule corresponding to the
heavy draught horses of Northern Europe, the equivalent of the

Shire and the Ardennais and the Jutland Horse, was bred in France, the sire being a special strain of jackass called 'Baudet de Poitou', and the dam a mare of Poitevin Mulassier draught breed.

Let us face it, the parents of the Poitevin mule are not beautiful by any standard. The Mulassière herself is distinguished by nothing but size. She does not move well out of a walk, she is long in the back, with thick, heavy head carried low, and sloping quarters, big, often lop, ears.

The Poitou jack has, for an ass, enormously thick bone below the knee and very broad feet. His back is also long; his coat is thicker at all times of the year than those of any other known breed—and it is curly, brown in colour and inclining to bay. The mane is also longer than in most breeds of donkey. The height is anything up to fifteen and a half hands.

Some idea of the scale and economic importance of Poitevin ass-breeding in its heyday at the end of the nineteenth century may be formed from the report made by Charles L. Sutherland to the Richmond Commission on Agriculture.

The Poitevin jackass, a variety as curious and perhaps as ugly as he is massive, short-legged and valuable, . . . is the most important of all quadrupeds in Poitou. He is the sire of the mules, and as such is the direct means of putting large sums of money into the pockets of the farmers. The price of a young improved animal of two years varies from £80 to £120; a good proved mule-getter, four year old, from 14 to 15 hands high, is worth from £200 to £320, and one was sold in the Vendée, just before the Franco-Prussian war, for £400. These valuable animals are kept in a filthy state, are never groomed, and never taken out of the building in which they are kept, except to be shown to a visitor or possible purchaser. The fee for the service of each mare is from 16s. to 20s. The female asses are rarely parted with, except for some defect. Their value may be set down at £24 to £40. The Conseil General of the Deux-Sèvres votes annually the sum of £200 for prizes for mules and asses at the local shows. These establishments are technically called *ateliers,* and the fact of owning such an establishment entitles the proprietor to the right to call himself *maître,* and gives him a position in the country. Each stud farm consists of from four to seven stallion asses, a stallion horse, a 'teaser', and one or more she-asses. The mares are also brought to the stud-farms, of which there are 160 in Poitou, the Deux-Sèvres alone claiming 94, with 465 jackasses.

The resultant mules were sold at three or four years old, in the
early months of the year, at fairs attended by dealers from all
over the South of France, from Spain, and from Italy; good ones
fetched £60 to £80, inferior ones half that sum. We must leave
the reader to translate the quotations in late Victorian pounds
into terms of whatever purchasing-power sterling may have on
the date when this work comes from the press. But even now,
the top price of £400 quoted above represents, certainly, more
than £1000 in contemporary currency.

Where this breed of ass originated, and whence its unique
characteristics are derived, it is hard to say. Traditionally the
foundation stock is held to have been brought from Catalonia,
but there is no documentary evidence for this, no oral tradition
about when the transplantation took place, and little similarity
except in point of height between the Poitevin and the Catalan.
We may examine here Hagedoorn's explanation of the unique
Poitevin characteristics, not because we accept it but because it
at least has been worked out in detail and coherently expressed
by a professional zoologist.

Expatriate Highland mercenaries at Mainz, 1743, with pack-mule
[*German Engraving, Scottish War Museum*

The Dutch geneticist A. L. Hagedoorn (1885–1953) not only worked on the problems of farm stock in Holland, France, the East Indies, and South Africa and had a doctor's degree from the University of California, he also had experience in Britain and Australia. His best-known work, *Animal Breeding*, was first published (by Crosby Lockwood) in 1939. The present quotations are from the sixth revised edition, 1962. His most striking claim for the mule in this book is as security guard. He says:

> in parts of Africa where horses are bred in country infested with leopards, on the open range, half a dozen mules added to the herd will effectively protect the younger foals, when the mares would be unable to cope with this great enemy. I have heard the same story from a professional hunter in the Californian puma country, where horse foals are also a favourite prey of the big cats!

Pack-mules of superior quality, detail from Gozzoli's
Journey of the Magi
[*Mansell Collection*

A general theme of his book is that it is easier to produce animals of uniform type, *in the first-generation cross*, by hybrid-breeding than by pure-line breeding, and speaking of mares used for mule-breeding in large establishments he says, "It is astonishing to see the enormous variety between the mares and the uniformity between the mule foals at any of the large markets where mule foals are bought and sold. The mares differ as much as horses can differ; the mules look as if they had been turned out by machinery."

He says that for some reason white and grey mules are very unpopular in some countries, and one wonders what country he means, since in the Middle East—an ancient homeland of the ass, which saw the first mule-breeding enterprises of the world's history—the white strain of donkey is the most prized of all.

> In French mule-breeding districts [he says] people believe that the donkey stallion should never be allowed to mate with donkey mares if he is to be used for mule breeding. All sorts of tricks are used to get the jack to serve a mare, from trying to make him jealous up to what is called 'le lalandage' in France. Anyone who has ever witnessed the ridiculous spectacle of a circle of stable-men joining hands and singing the aphrodisiacal "le-la-la" chorus around the hesitating stallion will be convinced with me that . . .

artificial insemination will save a lot of time and trouble. Maybe. But plainly this is a traditional, tried practical method we shall no longer be able to observe now that French mule-breeding is a thing of the past, and a very interesting example of the practical application of ancient fertility rites which were such a potent factor in the bygone religion of pastoral peoples. In such rituals—usually practised at the spring festivals—the ring of dancers with joined hands, singing at a pitch and in a rhythm whose erotic effect can be explained in terms of medicine as well as of psychology, was part of the procedure for ensuring fertility in more species than that of the ass.

He is speaking mainly of the Poitou district of France, and thinks that the giant ass known as *baudet de Poitou* has some horse-blood, introduced in the following way:

> Mules, at least some of the mares, are occasionally fertile; many instances have been described. The foals produced from the mating of such mares both with donkeys and back to the horse, have

been proved to be fertile again. . . . It should certainly be possible to use the fertile foals from fertile mare mules to start a breed of mules that would be fertile and would free the breeders from the continued species-cross. Whether it would pay to do this is not certain. . . .

(Hagedoorn was not really at home in the rarefied atmosphere of 'pure' science; his attitude was the down-to-earth one of the Dutch dirt-farmer.) He thought that the introduction of a slight dose of asinine genes into the horse-stock of South Africa would preserve the stock from hazards of climate and parasites, possibly also from epidemic diseases such as African Horse Sickness. Not only was he convinced of the desirability of this new line in breeding, but also that it was not new; that it had been done already, and that the larger French and Spanish strains of ass, and hence also the American Mammoth, were the result of a dash of horse in the heredity—how and where introduced, he did not venture to suggest. But from the evidence available, it seems to us that the evolution of a giant strain of ass by means of the drop-by-drop introduction of horse blood—and big-horse blood at that—would be a very costly and lengthy undertaking. It could only be done by way of mule mares, and the propagation of a new strain by means of female descent is always slower than the wrath of God. Consider only that a super-fertile, long-lived mare may give birth to twenty foals in her life, whereas a stallion can beget a thousand foals without the aid of artificial insemination. It is only a tiny proportion of mule mares that are fertile—one in many thousands—and the foal, if any, is always by a horse, not by a jackass. The foals born alive seem always to be female. They are perfectly well authenticated, and they probably seem more numerous than they really are, because as they are such freaks of nature every case gets the full publicity treatment. They are rare in England (but then mules are rare in England), but are otherwise evenly distributed throughout the world, from the officially reported case (photographs and all) on an Italian stud-farm in Libya between the wars to the sad affair of John T. Kilby's mule at Spring Hill, Nansemond County, Virginia, which had two female foals between 1834 and 1836; both by a horse, both fully reported in *The Farmer's Register*; neither lived to maturity. Whether in France or Spain, production of a stock of fertile hybrids large enough to produce a genetically stable new race would have involved many thousands of animals, would have been very costly because the proportion of rejects would be high, and would have been very slow, taking more than the life-time of one stud-owner to come within sight of its objective. Slower than we might otherwise think, because apart from the Kilby case we know of no mule-mare that has ever had more than one foal—the inference being that even those that are fertile are shy breeders. But given that the countries concerned are France and Spain, and that in Catholic Mediterranean Europe the riding-mule is regarded as the appropriate mount for an ecclesiastic, from the Pope downward, the obvious place for such an enterprise would be some estate in ecclesiastical ownership—the demesne of some bishopric, or of some monas-tic order distinguished, as the English Cistercian abbeys were before the Reformation, for their skill in stock-breeding. Such an establishment would be well equipped to undertake a long-term project like this, because, like a State stud, one 'manager' could succeed another without interrupting the programme. But this would also mean that in an age when the average farmer could neither read nor write, and the average landowner only did so under protest, and preferred to leave such matters to the professional cleric, the project would be taking place in the framework of an establishment where accounts were kept, where records of every kind were maintained from year to year, in cartularies and chronicles. In the absence of any such record we cannot credit the part-horse origin of giant asinine breeds.

It seems to us much more likely that the significant and sought-after features of the Poitevin ass have been produced 'from within'—that is, from within the asinine species, by mat-ing like with like, breeding from pairs both of which displayed points such as long hair, great height, etc., over a long period during which, though the search for suitable stock may have extended over a wide area, into Spain and possibly even farther afield, outcrossing has never extended beyond the bounds of the species *Equus asinus*.

The aversion to interbreeding between horses and donkeys in the wild is not, however, absolute. It probably only occurs when circumstances are such that the male sex of one species is totally absent for a time during the breeding season. This is

Poitevin mule-getting jackass
[*Scraper-board by Douglas Reay*

suggested by the fact that among some bands of feral ('gone-wild') mustangs in such areas as Colorado mule foals have been observed running with the mares. Such foals once grown up seem to be able to hold their own, and horses to have no 'racialist' prejudices; thus there was in the deserts of Nevada a band of mustangs the leader of which for many years was a white mule; when this animal was at length found dead, in 1965, it was found to be a female. And so, to hark back a little, though the biblical story of Anah and his wild mules is unlikely, it is shown by recent experience not to be totally impossible. One can, after all, 'find mules in the wilderness'!

Mule or hinny breeding is possible over the whole range of type and size, though for reasons stated below the smallest specimens are more likely to be hinnies, and a start has been made on the breeding of such 'fancy' miniatures in America, where coloured dwarf hinnies are currently being advertised for sale, being got by piebald Shetland stallions out of dwarf she-asses. But the most serviceable hinnies or jennets, of

Poitevin mare with mule foal
[*Scraper-board by Douglas Reay*

medium size, equal to that of the aboriginal wild horse and wild ass alike, are still to be found in the Mediterranean region which was the cradle of the race. A last stronghold of the ass and of the mule is the Mediterranean island of Cyprus, birth-place of Aphrodite and of Archbishop Makarios. The Cypriot ass, the Cypriot mule, and the Cypriot muleteer earned a con-siderable reputation in support of the British Army in two world wars, but long before this the asinine material of Cyprus was renowned for its high quality.

The figures of livestock published by the island's Department of Agriculture for 1967 are interesting to compare with those recorded and quoted on p. 66 as having returned from Baby-lonian captivity with the Children of Israel: a couple of hund-red more asses—6979 as opposed to 6720—about half the number of horses, but 873 mules as against the 245 owned by the Israelites in the time of Cyrus. In fact these figures need to be inflated by about one-fifth again because they refer only to Greek-Cypriot ownership. So we should read perhaps about 8370 asses, about 1050 mules, 375 horses, to include Turkish ownership. However, farmers on Cyprus, like farmers anywhere else, are somewhat circumspect in their attitude to officialdom. The census-recorder from the Department of Agriculture is to be feared, even though he is a Greek who may be bearing gifts in the form of subsidies, because behind him looms the gentle-man from the Inland Revenue who is all too keenly interested in one's means of livelihood. Probably the figure at the present day is therefore still over 12,000, asses and mules. But before the First World War about 7000 asses and nearly 1000 mules were exported from the island annually.

Mules proper are almost exclusively reserved in Cyprus for harness-work. Riding-animals and pack-animals are usually jennets, that cross of a stallion on a jenny which is rather despised in Western Europe, chiefly because it is usually out of a small jenny by a full-sized horse, and tends to disappoint by only reaching the stature of the distaff side. But as the jennies of Cyprus are good-sized animals of about thirteen hands, and are usually put to a wiry sort of pony stallion of much the same size, they produce offspring equal in height to both parents, with a very smooth gait to ride, and able to carry two hundred-weight on the local pattern of pack-saddle, which differs in design from that of the Greek mainland. It has never been the practice to export donkey mares, but to keep them all at home for breeding. The exports before 1914 were all jackasses and geldings. The jennets have about seven inch of bone below the knee, very flat, hard, dense bone like that of an Arab horse.

In England, while mule-breeding has never been of more than marginal importance, it has probably been practised, if only on a restricted scale, continuously since late Roman times. Place-names like Moulsoe in Berkshire, Moulscombe in Sussex, the Moultons in Cheshire, Lincolnshire, and Norfolk, Mulgrave in North Yorkshire, Muncaster (once Muleceaster) in the same county, and another of the same name in Cumberland, all date from the early days of the Saxon settlement and mean either 'mule farm' or the like, or else denote the estate of a man named Mūla. But Mūla itself is not an ordinary personal name but a nickname, meaning literally 'mule', and the only historical character with this name about whom we know any biographi-cal details was so called precisely because his mother was Welsh. Since such nicknames were never drawn from fantastic

or far-out images but from something earthily familiar (they
tend to mean 'Buck Teeth' or 'Bandylegs' or 'Wall Eye', etc.)
we may assume that these half-English characters called Mūla
owed their names to a not too uncommon farming practice of
the period. Of all these names, Muleceaster may be the most
significant, since the second element signifies a Roman building
of some sort (not necessarily a *castra* or fort). It is perhaps not
too fanciful to surmise that when the first Anglian settler established himself there it was in a Roman villa with mules in the
stables? Or at least that the locals gave him to understand that
that was what the stone-built stables had been used for?

For early Norman times the evidence is much more concrete.
For instance, in 1116 the Abbey of Burton-on-Trent kept thirty-
six brood mares and three Spanish jackasses. Obviously, with
such a stock the abbot was seriously involved in mule-produc-
tion.

English mule-breeding increased in quantity, but perhaps
not at all in quality, during the eighteenth century as the process of empire-building gained impetus. Canada excepted, the
new 'plantations' tended to be in hot countries where the mule
was more effective than the draught horses for farming purposes, and though the loss of the United States caused a set-
back, the ban on trade with colonies of other Powers (though
they might be adjacent) meant that Caribbean islands, for
instance, where mule-power was needed in the sugar-fields,
had to import English mules or breed their own. The real expansion of mule-breeding, where it was brought to a fine art by
persons of British descent took place in the United States, and
for that reason will be treated in the chapter partly devoted to
that country.

But wherever and whenever practised, mule-breeding is
such a complex business that it is remarkable it should have
been commenced, and carried out with success, so very early in
the history of man as a stock-breeder. For it demands threefold
skills. The product is ephemeral; it is impossible to establish
a 'line' of mules, and a new beginning must be made with every
generation, so that besides the expertise needed to arrange
the actual mating of pairs of animals of different temperaments,
and mostly of ill-matched size, it is necessary to maintain (if
the mules produced are to be of uniform type and quality) two

breeds with the desired qualities; a line of mares and a line of jackasses. This also brings economic problems in its train. Often, as in Poitou, the type of mare that will produce a 'good' daughter, who like herself will bear good mule foals, may bear colts (indeed, on average, will foal 50 per cent colts) that are not specially desirable as horses. Likewise, the jackass must be put to a certain number of jennies in order to provide successors to himself in the role of a sire of mules. But a use is unlikely to be found inside mule-breeding circles for that half of his progeny which are female; and of that half which are male only a small proportion will be needed for breeding. Therefore unless the country concerned uses a reasonable number of donkeys, wastage in the mule-breeding business will be rather high.

5 The Ass in Medieval Life and Legend

DURING the Middle Ages a sad decline took place in the status —though not in the numbers—of the ass in its old stronghold, the Middle East, and before we pass on to consider the part which this animal played in the popular imagination of Europe, it is worth while considering how it came to lose face on the other side of the Mediterranean.

From the middle of the ninth century of our era onward, leadership in the world of Islam began to fall from the hands of the Arabs; and though the Holy Book of all Mahomedans continued to be the untranslated Koran; though all Mahomedans of whatever race adopted personal names of Arabic form; though laws based on what was originally Bedouin tribal custom became current from Sinkiang to Morocco, the people who mattered in the Moslem world were mostly people of Turkish origin whose ancestors had been converted to Islam in the

Onager from English medieval bestiary
British Museum

campaigns of the eighth century. The Turks had belonged in
the distant past to the outer fringe of the horse-breeding tribes
whose centre was Mongolia; for immemorial ages they had been
a people who were born and lived and died on horseback, and
were closely related to the folk who had been the first of men
in all the world to tame the wild horse of the steppes.

How does it come about that in an Arab country such as Iraq,
one of the first Asiatic lands into which the ass was introduced
from North Africa, thousands of years before Mohammed's day,
it is at the present time impolite to utter the Arabic word for
'ass' unless it is at once neutralized by some deprecatory phrase
meaning 'if you will excuse me mentioning such a thing'? This
is entirely the result of Turkish influence. To the Turks the horse
was the ally that had brought them from the desolate fringes
of the Gobi desert to the riches of Bagdad, whose rulers they

French illuminated Gospel (fourteenth century). Miniature of Flight
into Egypt, with mule instead of ass (Arthaud, Grenoble)
[*British Museum*

had first served as mercenary cavalry and later deposed, after
manipulating them as puppets as long as it served their purpose. That ally would serve them well at the taking of Con-
stantinople, whose capture made them masters of all that was
left of the Roman Empire. It would stay with them, for that
matter, until they all but stormed Vienna, in the heart of
Europe. The Turk was never a peasant, never a merchant. His
occupation was either stock-breeding or warfare. Agriculture
and commerce, in an expanded Turkish kingdom, were the
occupations of the subject population. Thus in the Turkish-
dominated lands the ass was the servant of serfs. The Mongols
and the Tartars, of similar habit to the Turks, had the same
attitude ass-ward, and it was communicated to all the European peoples that had close contact with these horse-archers
of the Great Steppe, from the Danube to the Baltic. North of
a certain point the question hardly arises, since intense cold
stunts the growth and saps the strength of the ass in latitudes
where well-fed horses flourish. But even in climates which are
not at all unfavourable to the ass, such as Hungary, it is
regarded as of limited utility and no esteem—indeed, it has

Rhineland MS, c. 1312. Miniature of Nativity, with jennet
instead of traditional ass
[*The Metropolitan Museum of Art, The Cloisters Collection, 1968*

often been the chosen vehicle of insult and disgrace. For instance in Russia, so long under the dominion of the Tartars, the defeated Cossack rebel Stenka Razin was drawn to the place of execution on a sled behind four mules. In such countries, in such climates of opinion, the ass is the vehicle of the street-cleaner, and no attention is paid to mule-breeding. Indeed, the latter is most often the result of inadvertence; or if deliberate is the last artifice employed to start the reproductory mechanism going in a mare that has proved consistently barren to the horse.

Perhaps the use of the ass by ecclesiastics in countries where it was otherwise not often seen is a reminder of the fact that Christianity itself was something that came to us from Mediterranean lands in ages past. In the North of England the donkey figures in one of the few really cheerful stories (as opposed to legends) that illuminate the dreary chronicle of suffering and starvation under the first Norman kings. Here at Whitby, five years after the Harrying of the North, William the Conqueror's (or to use his more common Northern nickname, the Bastard's) all but totally successful attempt at genocide, the second founders of St Hilda's Abbey arrived, locating with some difficulty on the East Cliff what had been one of the two foremost monasteries in Northumbria. It was already some four centuries old. They were Reinfrid of Evesham, a Norman ex-soldier, and two Englishmen, Ealdwine of Winchcombe and Aelfwine the Deacon. The Abbey was in ruins, not for the first or the last time in its history. The pier was broken down, and the fishing-boats all stove in. As for the monks, not all of them were dead or fled across the Tees, but those who remained were completely demoralized, and had abandoned all semblance of communal life, each huddling in a separate corner of the desecrated buildings, withdrawn and introspective like hermits. Reinfrid and his comrades called on them to remember that they were Benedictines, not wharf-side rats, and to come out of their holes and start building. These energetic and courageous men had, according to Simeon of Durham, walked through the wolf-haunted forest and across the moors all the way from York, unarmed, with all their baggage carried on a single ass.

But in England the humble status of the ass seems to have been established from the moment of its introduction; that is, the Roman view of its worth was accepted without question.

At any rate, early in the Middle Ages we have an English interpretation of the Entry into Jerusalem in which the Hebrew association of the ass with royalty is not even guessed at. About a hundred years after the Norman Conquest there was not much written matter circulating in English. What there was was mainly for the use of the lower ranks of the clergy, such as the sealed-pattern sermons handed out in various sees for the benefit of those parish priests who could 'sing Mass', could read the Lessons in Latin, but were not too bright at composing their own pastoral addresses once a week. These hand-outs are called homilies, and usually comprise little more than an extended paraphrase, in English, of a portion of the Latin scriptures, with some commentary. The translation of a homily for Palm Sunday written perhaps in the reign of Henry II, and probably by the Bishop of Norwich (for it is in the Suffolk dialect of the time), reads

> Then He sent two of His disciples into the town of Jerusalem and told them to fetch Him a mount to ride on. Neither steed, nor palfrey, nor fair mule, although He was lord of all lords and king of all kings; nevertheless He sent for the most undignified of all mounts to ride on, namely an ass.[1]

So there it is, spelt out. That is what the ass meant to the Englishman, and indeed to all Europeans north of the Alps, in the day of the Crusaders. By contrast the mule is mentioned in the same breath as the elegant palfrey and the expensive military 'steed'—the English word for what the Normans called a destrier. One would expect to see a bishop or an abbot riding a 'fair mule'.

This was also the conventional view in Scotland, where the donkey was much rarer. In the *Kingis Quair*, by James I of

----

[1] This Old English Homily, probably in the Suffolk district, and dating before 1200, reads in the original:

Palm Sunday

Tho the com to Beth fage (swo hatte the throp the preste on wunien) bisides Ierusalem on the fote of the dune the men clepen Munt Olivete. Tho sende tweyen of his discipules into the bureh of Ierusalem and bed hem bringen a wig on to riden. Nother stede, ne palefrei, ne fair mule, ac theh he were alre lauerdes lauerd and alre kingene king, natheles he sende after the alre unwurthest wig on to riden, and that is asse.

Scotland—long an exile, and a hostage of the English, one of
the menagerie of prominent political prisoners that Henry IV
kept in the Tower of London—it figures as

> The slawe as, druggar beste of pyne

which, rendered out of the difficult spelling and vocabulary of
Middle Scots, means 'the slow ass, drudging beast of labour'.

The ass hardly enters into the folk-lore of temperate Europe
before the Middle Ages for the simple reason that down to that
time the animal itself was unfamiliar in real life outside the
confines of what had been the Roman Empire. Even as hearsay,
it only became known to the Northern peoples as a by-product
of the spread of Christianity. Thus it is associated with legends
of St Nicholas, whose feast falls early in December, and who
has attracted in lands around the North Sea some of the attributes of a Nordic Winter God; with St Martin of Tours, whose
Day is celebrated on November 11th, at the onset of winter,
and who also assumed in legend some of the attributes of the
forgotten gods of pagan Gaul. In France the donkey is popularly
named Martin after him, just as in Northumberland it is called
Cuddy, after Cuthbert, the Saint of Holy Island, whose cult
was once of immense importance throughout Northumbria.

Miller's pack-ass. Illumination in English bestiary
[*British Museum*

By association with these holy men, it came to play a considerable part in folk-medicine, its blood being regarded as a cure for jaundice, and its hairs as a specific remedy for whooping-cough. A poultice of Ass-dung was prescribed by 'wise women' for 'dimness' of the eyes (probably either cataract or trachoma), while gout was treated by tying the right hoof of an ass to the left leg of the patient, and vice versa.

Christian folk-lore of the ass outside the Mediterranean regions came to the fore in the winter months, possibly as an antidote for gloom, as being a creature with still some aura of the sunny South. At any rate, it was concentrated, in Flanders and Northern France, in the Feast of the Ass, which was celebrated in the middle of January. This began as a simple acting out of a scriptural chapter appropriate to the weeks following Christmas, the Flight into Egypt, and was a Miracle Play like any other, having as leading characters in the cast a girl with a baby in arms mounted on an ass, which was led around the churchyard. At Beauvais it assumed its most elaborate form, and later degenerated into a burlesque of the same kind, though not as sinister, as those which members of the witch cult enacted in their Sabbat: a parody of the Mass. After the symbolic Journey to Egypt outside, the procession came into the church, and the actors, including the donkey, partook of a meal off a specially furnished table, while the priest and congregation danced round them, hee-hawing. After that farces were played, outside the building, until late in the evening. The day ended with a midnight Mass, normal in all respects except that at the end, when the priests should have pronounced the words *Ite, missa est* he brayed "Hee-haw, hee-haw, haw", and the congregation brayed at him by way of Amen. Real live asses also figured, though more decorously, in religious mime celebrating Palm Sunday, and in some countries where no such animals existed, but were known principally from the pictures in missals and gospels drawn from life in more southern lands, elaborate arrangements were made to simulate 'a colt, the foal of an ass'. Thus in Moscow, where in the Middle Ages there were no asses or mules (though they were to be found in Southern Russia), the Orthodox Patriarch himself enacted the role of the Saviour, and his mount was led by the Grand Duke in person. But the mount was invariably a horse, covered entirely by a white housing with 'sleeves' for the legs, and having large ears stiffened with whalebone or something similar, fitted over the real ears.

An English traveller to Moscow writing as late as 1557 says:

> On Palm Sunday they have a very solemn procession in the manner following: first, there is a horse covered with white linen cloth down to ye ground, *his ears being made long* with ye same cloth like to an asses eares. Upon this horse the Metropolitan [of Moscow] sitteth sidelong like a woman; in his lappe lieth a faire book, with a crucifix of goldsmith's work on the cover, which he holdeth fast with his left hand, and in his right hand he hath a cross of gold, with which crosse he ceaseth not to bless the people as he rideth. There are to the number of 30 men which spred their garments out before the horse as soon as the horse is passed over any of them, they take them up againe and run before, and spred them againe, so that the horse doth alway go in front of them. They which spred their garments are all priests sons, and for their labour the Emperor giveth unto them new garments. One of the Emperours noble men leadeth the horse by the head, but the Emperour himself goth on foot, leadeth the horse by the rein of his bridle with one of his hands and in the other of his hands he hath the branch of a palm tree. . . .

It is interesting to see that the pageant-master knew enough about Near Eastern matters not only to dress the horse with long, ass-like ears but to drape it in white, to simulate the Damascene milk-white breed of ass used in the East for ceremonial purposes, and no doubt on the original Palm Sunday.

Striking proof of the innocence of the donkey in terms of popular belief is implied in the purely negative evidence of witch trials. While most of the court records that we have of trials for witchcraft belong to the seventeenth century, the very spate of prosecutions for this offence in England, Scotland, France, and other Western countries was part of the process of shedding the rags of medieval custom, and there is no doubt at all that witchcraft was one of the living realities for a large sector of the population throughout the Middle Ages. The Devil was wont to appear to the assembled witches in the guise of a he-goat most of the time, but numerous other animal disguises were also used—sometimes a stag, a ram, or a bull. On several occasions a black horse or pony ("ane blak galoway" in more than one Scottish transcript of proceedings) was the form assumed

by the Devil; that is, the ritual disguise adopted by the local
leader of the cult. But almost never was the disguise a donkey.
A close approach to the asinine devil appears in a legend of
the time of Charlemagne, noted in the life of that emperor by
Notker the Stammerer: a certain Italian bishop was persuaded
by a miser to buy from him what seemed to be a very fine
mule, at a quite exorbitant price. But the mule was in fact the
Devil in disguise, and the whole thing a put-up job between
him and the miser, part of the usual bargain whereby Satan
buys the soul of some sinner by undertaking to make him very
rich in this world, and never mind the hereafter. No sooner had
the bishop spat in his hand than he set out to show off his new
purchase, which after peacocking through the cathedral city
bolted across country and ran up to his neck into a river with the
bishop on board, then swam up and down 'like a school of
dolphins'. The rider was only saved by the intervention of some
fishermen.

It is arguable, of course, that the donkey is excluded from
the setting of witchcraft (which only assumed the form which
is familiar to us in Northern Europe) because of the very
antiquity of such beliefs. They go back to a time when people
this side of the Alps did not know there was such a thing as a
donkey. The same reasoning applies to the rarity of the donkey
in English, German, Dutch, or Scandinavian folk-tales. Where
it does appear it is probably a comparatively late substitute for
some other beast. In these popular stories each animal has its
characteristic traits, which hardly vary from story to story; the
wolf personifying greed, the fox cunning, and so on. The ass is
shown as the one who can endure all things for a long time,
who is impervious to insult and indignity and blows, because
he knows that sooner or later his turn will come.

Yet again, touching the innocence of the ass. In the peasant
traditions of the North of England there is found the belief in a
variety of spectres of animal form, which may go back in
essence to the beliefs of North-countrymen in Celtic times—
say the Brigantes. The animal can belong to one of several
species, from the Barguest of Lancashire, which was a black,
silent, spectral hound with luminous eyes, that trotted at the
heels of travellers on lonely roads, to the Geytrash of Goath-
land, in the North Riding, a ghostly billy-goat of malevolent

aspect. Often this unearthly beast was a horse—black, needless to say. But in one instance, unique so far as I know, it assumed asinine form. This was at Pelton, in County Durham, where a not particularly lonely byway called Pelton Lonin' was haunted by The Brag, a harbinger of death. It too was sometimes like a "black galloway", but an old lady who saw it about 1750 said that it was 'like a dick-ass'. A jackass is a dick-ass in Durham— the only other county that shares this expression with East Anglia—whereas a Durham cuddy can be of either sex.

To most Northern peasants the ass was simply a stage-property in a variety of Bible stories—which of course they did not read, but had read out to them by the parson once a week. But there was not only the oral medium. The Church thought up the visual-aid technique long before modern educational systems came to exploit it. There were the elaborately illuminated gospels and psalters for the rich, custom-made like the Holkham Picture Bible or the Luttrell Psalter, certainly never looked into by a poor man. But there were also the fresco paintings on the interior walls of the churches, only a handful of which survived the Reformation. However, before about

Tuscany in the fourteenth century, with pack-asses and mules. Detail from Domenico Lorenzetti, *Il Buon Governo*
[*Photo Grassi, Siena*

1540 the parish churches in England which had almost every flat space on their interior walls covered with fresco or tempera paintings of biblical subjects (of very varying merit) greatly outnumbered those which had not such sacred comic strips.

These paintings gave the artist with a penchant for asinine subjects much more scope than the limner who specialized in horses. In the New Testament the latter has only the Kings Journeying to Bethlehem, and the Four Horsemen of the Apocalypse, on which to exercise his skill. In the Old, only a passage from the Book of Job, a very odd verse or two from Zechariah, some terrifying sentences from Habbakuk—and that is about all. By contrast, there is a wealth of material in which donkeys figure, and it is all important. The Sacrifice of Isaac, for instance. Joseph and his brethren and their adventures in Egypt. Balaam and his talking jenny. Saul looking for the strayed asses of his father Kish, and finding a kingdom. These and many more were the scenes that adorned the church walls.

To these pictures must be attributed the very gradual intrusion of the ass into the Nativity story. Modern retellings of the Christmas story, no matter whether in Catholic or in Protestant communities, mention asses among the inmates of that stable in Jerusalem, and nine modern Christmas cards out of every ten showing the Nativity include an ass. Not even St Luke's Gospel mentions any such animal in its most circumstantial account of the Nativity itself. How then did it get to the centre of the stage so early? The earliest mention I can find in English is this snatch of a fourteenth-century carol:

> In a simple hous,
> A povre stable, mong bestes reweless,
> An ox, an ass, no coursers costious,
> In a streyht rakke lay ther the kyng of pees.

"Coursers costious" means 'expensive race-horses'. The verse is inspired almost certainly less by reading the Gospel or by hearing it read than by looking at the pictures on the walls of the nave, or possibly at an illuminated Bible. All English, and probably all Northern, Bible pictures are derivative, they are new treatments of subjects first studied in books of Italian or other Mediterranean origin. Quite early on it became the fashion in England to dress the Wise Men of the East not as

Persian mystics but as crowned kings on horseback. But the Adoration of the Shepherds was much more faithfully copied. Shepherds abiding in the field, in the real-life Galilee of the first century, would have their donkeys with them as a matter of course, and it would be the most natural thing in the world to ride away on them in pursuit of that star. So it would be in Italy, both in early Christian times and for long after. As we shall see, in a later chapter, the donkey is as essential to the Provençal shepherd as is the dog to the Scottish or Welsh shepherd even now. In spite of the fact that in England there is no traditional association between the donkey and the shepherd, and never has been, early English artists faithfully copied the donkeys and their gear from Italian pictures of the Adoration of the Shepherds, and only gradually did these become detached from their owners and figure as the regular inhabitants of the "povre stable" of our card.

Where for many centuries the difference between England and the Continent in the matter of donkeys really lay was chiefly this. Ever since Roman times, when corn was ground either by hand in 'querns' or in mills operated by donkeys, the Continental ass was most often seen in some job connected with milling. If it were not actually operating the mill (as it operated the wine-press and the olive-press in the South) it would be carrying grain to the mill or meal away from it. This was a job that went on steadily, using fairly small quantities, from one harvest-time round to another, because whole grain keeps so much better than flour. A donkey-load was a convenient quantity for the large household to have ground at one time, and the majority of asses belonged either to millers or to the farmers whose grist they ground. But not, for some reason, in England. Even in Norfolk, traditionally the home of the dickie (pronounced dicker), and the county in which the English ass has been longest acclimatized, it seems that the weekly traffic to and from the mill was always entrusted to a pack-horse.

6 *The Donkey in New Worlds*

ROYAL GIFT

A JACK ASS of the first race in the Kingdom of Spain will cover
mares and jennies at Mount Vernon the ensueing spring. The
first for ten and the latter for fifteen pounds the season. Royal
Gift is four years old, is between 14½ and 15 hands high, and
will grow, it is said, till he is 20 or 25 years old. He is very
bony and stout made, of a dark colour, with light belly and
legs. The advantages, which are many, to be derived from the
propagation of asses from this animal (the first of the kind that
ever was in North America) and the usefulness of mules bred
from a Jack of his size, either for the road or team, are well
known to those who are acquainted with this mongrel race. For
the information of those who are not, it may be enough to add
that their great strength, longevity, hardiness and cheap support, give them a preference of horses that is scarcely to be
imagined. As the Jack is young, and the General has many
mares of his own to put to him, a limited number only will be
received from others, and these entered in the order they are
offered. Letters directed to the subscriber, by Post or otherwise,
under cover to the General, will be entered on the day they are
received, till the number is completed, of which the writers
shall be informed to prevent trouble or expense to them.
    John Fairfax
      Overseer.   Feb 23, 1786.

THE above advertisement, in a Philadelphia newspaper, was
inserted on behalf of General George Washington, who had
gone to considerable trouble to procure this fine Catalonian
jack. There had been mules in America before the Revolu-
tionary War, but they were probably of inferior quality, and
certainly of rather small size. They were not bred in the colonies
but imported 'ready-made' from England. The principal source
had been the New Forest in Hampshire, where commoners who
had grazing rights in the forest had been in the habit of run-

Maltese Jackass, c. 1800. Contemporary engraving

ning a few jackasses along with the ponies which grazed there.
Whether these mares produced a pony foal or a mule foal was
probably a matter of chance most of the time: it depended who
got there first—a New Forest pony stallion or a jackass. As it
is the size of the dam which determines that of the offspring,
and as the average New Forest mare of those days was seldom
above thirteen hands high, these mules would have been more
the size that nowadays we associate with jennets—that is,
hybrids out of donkey mares. Nor was the conformation at all
pleasing, since most of the jackasses kept on the Forest were
not of high quality. We reproduce (p. 106) the common sort of
New Forest jackass then siring the run-of-the-mill mules, and a
very superior mule occasionally arose, the product of a good
jackass and the better sort of New Forest mare; but these
would be exceptional. However, these animals were cheap,
since they were reared on free grazing, and the New Forest

lies convenient to Southampton and Portsmouth, so that there would be no expense in travelling them to the port of embarkation.

But now the bad old colonial days were over. It was up to the citizens of the new republic to see what they could do on their own, and their first President gave them a lead, even before his inauguration.

He therefore wrote to the King of Spain, Charles IV, requesting permission to buy some Spanish asses of the best quality. Since at that period Spanish exports as well as imports were rigidly controlled, the King avoided establishing a commercial precedent by making a free gift of two of either sex to the President. Only one jack, Royal Gift, and the two jennies survived the Atlantic crossing and arrived at Mount Vernon in December 1785.

New Forest ass for siring mules for export to America, c. 1786
Plate from W. Gilpin, *Remarks on Forest Scenery* (1791)

Next year Washington's old comrade-in-arms, the Marquis de Lafayette, sent him a Maltese jack, thus putting him in possession of specimens of the two leading European strains, though Knight of Malta was not as tall as Royal Gift, and his ears were only twelve inches long. At Mount Vernon a strain of asses was bred, via a jack of mixed Spanish-Maltese ancestry, called appropriately 'Compound'.

General Shelby, writing some sixty years after the "Knight of Malta's" landing, and quoted as an expert in mule-breeding, said, "The Maltese jack of fourteen hands I consider entitled to the same rank and dignity in his race that is accorded to the Arabian Horse in his". Of the 'Compound' strain he says, "a cross between [the Maltese] and the Spanish jack of sixteen hands will be found to combine all the essential properties of size, form and action, and to facilitate the breeding of mules possessing these requisites".

Jacks of either breed had been sold in Kentucky, a foremost mule-breeding state, at prices as high as 5000 dollars before 1840.

Pit-head, probably in Durham, early nineteenth century, with asses carrying (?) firewood
[*Walker Art Gallery, Liverpool*

For a long time American experts were sharply divided in their allegiance as between the Maltese party and the Spanish party. However, from the fact that the latter often used to describe their favourite animal as 'the Spanish or French jack', and to describe it as sixteen hands high, there seems to have been some confusion in their minds as between the true Spanish (Catalan or Andalusian) race and the Poitou. The latter was undoubtedly derived from Spanish (among other) ancestors, but equally undoubtedly attained its final size and other characteristics while bred in France. It is from this Poitou breed that the American Mammoth breed—which quite often reaches a stature of sixteen hands—is derived. A typical supporter of the Maltese breed, G. W. P. Custis, of Arlington, Virginia, who remembered the two protagonists in their lifetime, wrote:

> The GIFT was a huge and ill-shaped jack, near sixteen hands high, very large head, clumsy limbs, and to all appearance calculated for active service. He was of a grey colour, probably not young when imported, and died at Mount Vernon but little valued for his mules, which were unwieldy and dull.
> The KNIGHT was of a moderate size, clean limbed, great activity, the fire and ferocity of a tiger, a dark brown, nearly a black colour, white belly and muzzle, could be managed only by one groom, and that always at considerable personal risk. . . . *His* mules were all active, spirited and serviceable, and from stout mares attained considerable size.

After the Knight several more jacks were brought to the United States direct from the island, some in merchant shipping and some by the officers of naval frigates—a by-product of the expedition against the Barbary corsairs of Tripoli. But Spanish stock was harder to get for a long time. The afore-mentioned embargo on exports was not lifted until 1813. Theoretically it applied also to the Spanish colonies, but in practice a fair number of donkeys were smuggled over from what remained of the Spanish islands in the Caribbean (mostly from Cuba). However, life in the humid, sub-tropical, insular climate had played havoc with them genetically, and they were not a patch on the original Iberian stock. Apart from this, jacks of the pure Spanish strain were used to get mules for heavy draught, Maltese jacks for riding and carriage mules. From Virginia both kinds, as well as the Compound, spread rapidly all over the southern states, but made less headway in the north, both for climatic reasons and also because Negro drivers and grooms did better with mules than did white men, while before the Civil War and its aftermath Negroes were somewhat of a rarity in the northern states.

Royal Gift did not only stand at Mount Vernon. He travelled, like any thoroughbred stallion, but his powers on his first stud tour were grossly overtaxed. Washington wrote to a kinsman in South Carolina, Colonel William Washington:

> in Virginia, Royal Gift was most abominably treated on the journey, by the man [John Fairfax?] to whom he was entrusted for, instead of moving him slowly and steadily along, first of all he was prancing the jack from one public meeting to another, in a gait which could not but prove injurious to the animal, who had barely been out of a walk before, and afterward I presume in order to recover lost time, he was rushed beyond what he was able to bear the remainder of the journey.

The amount of the stud fee in the advertisement quoted is interesting. "The season" presumably means one heat. There are plenty of jacks standing today in England £10 and £15, and few owners would charge more than this unless they undertook to cover the mare again if she 'turned' the first time round, or even the second, without further charge except for keep. So this is a field in which no significant inflation seems to have taken place over nearly two centuries.

The climatic pattern affecting distribution of the ass and the mule in the New World seems to have reproduced with fair fidelity that of the Old World. Ideal conditions for the donkey in the ancestral African continent lay between 30 and 35 degrees North; thus acclimatization in Mediterranean Europe was easy. South of this tolerable conditions are only found on the east side of the continent, about 10 degrees North (Somaliland), until one reaches to about 20 degrees South, whence good conditions extend all the way to the Cape of Good Hope. That of the Asiatic races of wild ass is more northerly, and overlaps much more with that of the wild horse, which extends from about 40 to 55 degrees North.

German picnic on donkey-back, 1775. Engraving after
Daniel Chodowiecki

In terms of the United States, 40 degrees, the northern boundary of Kansas and (approximately) Maryland seems to mark the natural northern limit of ass country. The greater part of the American continent, therefore, suitable for keeping asses without special provision for wintering lay by a wide margin in what was once Spanish territory, and this is reflected in the distribution of the ass and mule population as a whole over the continent today.

In Latin America the spread of the ass and the breeding of mules has been limited by the presence of a competitor not found in other continents, but even more suitable than asses or mules for work at high altitudes—those South American camels, the llama and the alpaca. These animals, however, can in fact only carry the half (about 120 pounds) of what both continents over the centuries have regarded as the standard horse or mule load, and they are much less suitable for riding and draught than for pack-work. In a southern latitude corresponding to that of Somaliland, the very fine asses and mules of Peru are found, and the distance from the equator and the altitude together may account for their superiority, since as we saw in the first chapter there is reason to believe that domestic-ass foundation stock may once have included a measurable Somali element mingled with the predominant Nubian ancestry; indeed, colour variations tend to bear this out. At 35 degrees South lies the island of Tristan da Cunha, where donkeys flourish in a horseless land, and on the same parallel the Argentine mule, once produced and exported in large numbers for military purposes, is still of some economic importance, though we tend to think of Argentina primarily as a horse country.

Although the first wave of English-speaking settlers on the Atlantic coast were predominantly of East Anglian origin—that is, they came from a part of England where the rainfall is comparatively low, and where asses in the seventeenth century were rather plentiful—they do not appear to have brought any with them, and the great majority of North American asses appear to be ultimately of Iberian stock. Meanwhile, South of the Border, donkey business had been going on down Mexico way since long before the first White Anglo-Saxon Protestant waded ashore. If the humble request made in 1521 by Bishop Sebastian Ramirez de Funleal, Governor of New Spain, to His Christian Majesty for 300 jennies to be given to the Indians was not granted, at least in 1531 twelve jennies and

African asses on offshore island of Lanzarote, Canaries, near the African coast. Plough team under yoke as alternative to camel

three jacks were sent, and not given to the Indians straight
away, though eventually some asses did find their way into
Redskin ownership. Here be it noted that the Red Indians *as a
whole* never took to the ass and the mule on the same scale or
in the same spectacular way as they did to the horse. The horse
mania which ran through the aboriginal tribes like wildfire
within less than two centuries, from the Mississippi to the
Pacific, transformed them from pedestrian dog-drivers, who
either subsisted on small game or grew beans and maize to sup-
plement a main diet of roots and wild fruits, into full-time
nomadic hunters of the buffalo engaged in perpetual warfare,
either against each other (for reasons solely of prestige) or
against the Palefaces (for reasons—which did not come off—of
survival). Before 1680 there were virtually no mounted Indians.
By 1890 the last organized resistance to the U.S. Cavalry by
mounted Indian warriors was over, and their breeding herds
were dispersed and brought to nothing within a decade after
that. But some tribes in Mexico, like the Pueblos (who lived a
village life dependent on settled agriculture, not unlike that of
certain Mediterranean countries), did adopt the donkey, which
fitted in admirably with their economy.

It seems probable that the donkey-stock of the United States
as a whole is derived less from the rather carefully-bred Found-
ing Fathers of the Atlantic Seaboard, the Sons of Compound,
than from a steady infiltration from across the Rio Grande,
largely by way of trade between Spanish-speaking and English-
speaking Americans, but also by the medium of the Indians,
who will thus have played the same part in distribution as
did the gipsies in the South of England, or as did the Scottish
tinkers in distributing a certain type of Galloway pony throughout the North of England during much the same period.

There is no breed of ass that can be regarded as a specific
and original American development, least of all the 'American'
Spotted Burro. The stately sixteen-hand (well, occasionally)
American Mammoth has had this claim made for it.

However, the American Mammoth breed must obviously be
derived from the largest and most massive European variety,
the Poitou. The next senior group of colonists to the English
and Scots, the Dutch, came from a country where the donkey
was known but not common or highly esteemed, and neither

they nor the early German immigrants into such states as Pennsylvania (also confusingly called 'Dutch' in early records) seem to have brought any asses with them. Large numbers of New Americans did not begin to arrive in the States from classic ass-breeding Mediterranean lands such as Greece and Sicily until late in the nineteenth century, and they were mostly too poor to bring anything with them but the clothes they stood up in and a burning desire to do better for themselves and their children than their parents had been able to do for them. The same is true of the Irish, displaced by famine and the mal-administration of their country in the 1840s and later; on the whole, these also arrived broke and mokeless.

The general trend, then, in the United States has been the penetration of the country from south to north by asses from the Spanish sphere of influence, a penetration very slow at first, but gathering momentum as the Spanish settlement of Mexico became independent and expanded northward, towards the final confrontation (in what was to become Texas) with other settlers from the north-east. But at the same time there was a steady progression westward, both of donkeys and mules. The covered wagons that carried the settlers across the great plains towards Oregon were sometimes drawn by horses, some-times by oxen, and sometimes by mules. In more arid country the father of the mule came into his own. Deserts, historically speaking, were no novelty to him. What the donkey had done long ago on the caravan routes across the Sahara he performed again in American deserts and semi-deserts, carrying not only water, which he himself drank so abstemiously, but the tools, the provisions, and the bedding of hard-bitten prospectors in search of every sort of exploitable mineral—not only of the gold that makes the headlines. Like the horse, the donkey became the chosen vehicle of certain Red Indian tribes, and like the horse he reverted on occasion to nature, so that side by side with the mustangs—wild horses of domestic origin—there exist and have existed herds of wild asses which are descended from American-owned tame asses.

Texas, New Mexico, Arizona (which it would be cruel to call an arid zone): these are the typical American 'donkey' states, where the pure-bred *Equus asinus* is equally as important as its hybrid progeny, and its territory reaches north into California and Nevada and Colorado. North of this comes a belt of 'mule country'. East of the Mississippi, the plantation economy of the Deep South, with its emphasis on cotton and corn (maize) would have been unworkable in pre-mechanical days without abundant Negro labour and myriads of mules. The pre-eminence which Kentucky enjoyed in the early nineteenth century as a mule-breeding state was ascribed by a leading mule-man of the period to the surplus of maize which the state produced; this is a cereal on which the mule thrives, and can work all day with only the addition of chaffed straw as a bulk fodder. Horses not in work, on the other hand, can be fed maize in moderation, but it is too fattening and too heating to supply their entire corn ration, and for bulk they must have hay, and good hay at that. Ohio, Indiana, and Illinois are also mule country, which is continued across the Mississippi through Missouri, Arkansas, Oklahoma, and Kansas. Beyond the 40th parallel North climatic factors come into play, and even more so in Canada. If there are mules in the northern states most of them have been imported from the South. Only recently has the mule been naturalized in the most northerly state of the Union. A business concern in Alaska recently advertised for—and got, through the medium

Wild-fowlers, with the rare British jennet: James Ward, c. 1826
[*Tate Gallery*

of the special-interest Press—a sizeable team of draught mules
and skilled operators to work them in that sub-arctic climate.

In the opening up of the West the mule played a vital part,
in the service of what in England is called the civil engineer. In
the construction of roads and railways across the plains and
the Rockies vast mileages of carriage-way were graded, long
before the days of the bulldozer, by draglines, scrapers, and
other contrivances powered by teams of mules.

In the Indian wars, without which Hollywood might never
have achieved its output of epics for sheer lack of material, the
mule played an equally vital part. The United States cavalry
columns did not live off the country, they had to be supplied
like any other army, even if they did not require as part of their

Dutch herdsmen with pack-ass, by Aelbert Cuyp (1620–1691)
[*National Gallery of Art, Washington, D.C.*

logistical support the mobile ice-cream plants and the Field
Mortician Parlours that keep the modern doughboy and his
momma happy . . . well, willing to keep on with the war, anyway. What you never see on the films, along with the whooping
Nez Percés or Navajos and the fire-spitting Remingtons and
Gatlings, is the organization that made the whole thing tick—
the Cavalry Mule Train. These trains followed up the fighting
echelon across country impassable to wheeled traffic, as close
as was tactically possible; and indeed great tactical skill was
needed by the Train Master to keep near enough to the cavalry-
men to replenish their cartridge pouches and their stomachs as
often as necessary, while at the same time not exposing his
pack-mules to the depredations of a highly mobile enemy, who
was always capable of making a deep raid on the lines of
communication. The classic work on the organization and
handling of animal transport on active service—even better
than the old War Office manual *Animal Management*—was
written by an officer who had commanded one of these Mule
Trains. It is so informative that we reproduce parts of it in an
Appendix. Suffice it to say here that it was manned, in the late
nineteenth century, by civilians, as the Commissary's Branch
of the British Army had been up to the time of the Crimean
War. But such civilians! Ex-cowboys, ex-miners, ex-lumber-
men; civilians seasoned by the mountains and the forests and
the deserts. And all dedicated mule-men.

Hunting, in America, means the pursuit of game by any and
every means, principally with firearms. In its narrower English
sense, involving the use of hounds, it is practised only in certain
narrowly restricted parts of the United States, and in some of
these (Kentucky, Tennessee, West Virginia) the mule plays a
leading role. Raccoon-hunting takes place in the woods on moon-
lit nights. In that enormous stress is laid on the melodious music
of hounds, it resembles nothing so much as old English hare-
hunting. When treed by hounds, the 'coon is shot by the hunter,
but in order to do this he must first get his target silhouetted
against the moon, as English villains (or villeins) do with roost-
ing pheasants. The actual pursuit, however, is conducted on
mules, and a good jumping mule is required. Apart from fallen
trees and the like, the obstacles consist of barbed-wire fences
which are jumped from a stand. The Kentucky hunting-man

carries with him a square of tarpaulin, preferably white. On meeting wire he dismounts, unfolds his tarpaulin and spreads it over the top wire, partly to protect the mule's shins and partly to give him something solid to measure with his eye . . . an artificial baseline and crest-line.

Since the memory of the great services rendered to the pioneers by the ass and the mule is so vivid, and the events are so recent, the American revival in prestige for these two animals has taken place at a time when a sizeable minority of rural Americans are still earning their living by their aid.

Thus societies for their protection, improvement, welfare, uplift—what you will—contain not only amateurs but an honest commercial vested interest. There is not only the American Donkey and Mule Society, whose motto is, "They Helped Build Our Country"—nationwide, but with its administrative nerve-centre in Denton, Texas—but also an entirely pure-breed society, the American Council of Spotted Asses, and local bodies like the Ohio Wagon Train Association, whose delight is to assemble at week-end rallies for the purpose of driving four-in-hand teams of mules to Conestoga or 'covered' wagons. There is also a Society for the Protection of Mustangs and Burros whose objects will be dealt with later.

Ass in Lanarkshire farmyard, by James Howe (1780–1836)
[*Photo Tom Scott, Edinburgh*

Donkey races take place in some Western states (*e.g.*, annually at Beatty, Nevada) and there are also mule races, in harness. The pacing horse exists in the States, at least as frequently as the *paso fino* in Latin America, under two guises; first as that sort of sulky-racing Standard-bred which paces where other harness-racing horses trot, and secondly as the American Saddle Horse, which paces among other show gaits. But the pacing mule is not deliberately bred, as it is south of the Rio Grande. However, mule foals out of pacing mares are of course just as likely to pace as are their dams. The most famous pacing mule of all, Old Salem, was foaled in 1873 at Sycamorah Plantation, near Rienzi, Missouri. And he was chance-bred, in a manner of speaking. Some young sparks thought to play a trick on Tom Hinton of Sycamorah by letting a jack donkey into his brood-mare paddock one dark autumn night. Next October, his valuable pacing mare Highland Fling foaled a mule which was duly broken to harness and used in cultivation on the plantation. He was, incidentally, chestnut, an unusual colour in mules. The hands on Hinton's estate soon found out that he had a great propensity for fast pacing, and in their leisure time drove him, more or less clandestinely, in their own buggies, which they raced against each other. He beat a great many of their trotting horses. Finally he came out into the open, and in a series of matches against the best pedigree trotters and pacers over a one-mile course he beat all comers from Mississippi, Alabama, and Tennessee. At that time it was the custom among harness racers to decide the match on the best out of three successive one-mile heats. Old Salem was sold, to go to Texas in 1879.

In the Rocky Mountain states mules still run in competitive trail rides and marathons over difficult country, and acquit themselves well against horses. Here the opposition consists not so much of Thoroughbred or half-bred rivals but either of pure-bred Arabs, part-bred Arabs, or Quarter horses.

It is in these mountainous regions that the greatest ethical and practical problem has arisen concerning the American donkey. Inevitably, the automobile and the tractor and the truck have rendered a great many horses and donkeys redundant, and these have gone to swell the already appreciable numbers of donkeys and horses that over the centuries have

AMERICAN COUNCIL OF SPOTTED ASSES
"PUT COLOR IN YOUR LIFE"

ACE REID

Spotted Ass Promoter

Membership card of American Council of Spotted Asses

strayed from white or Indian ownership and run wild. On the plains the herds of feral horses that once were comparable in numbers with the buffalo have become even more extinct than the latter; totally so, in fact, since there are still some thousands of buffalo (American bison) in reserves, and their numbers are on the upgrade. But the mountains have become the last refuge of the mustang, and also of the burro. *Burro* (and its diminutive *burrito*) is the ordinary Spanish term for a general-utility ass, but in 'Western' English it has come to mean (*a*) a Mexican-bred ass, and thence (*b*) more specifically, the descendants of the same, run wild. The Great Plains were deliberately cleared of mustangs and burros by ranchers anxious to preserve all the grass there was for the benefit of their cattle and sheep—simply a matter of eliminating the competitive grazers, part of the process in which the buffalo and the antelope and the white-tailed deer vanished from the prairie scene. Now, the last stronghold of the mustang and the burro is in the higher ranges of the mountains, where neither cattle nor sheep can be economically kept, and they only compete for grazing with game animals like the big-horn sheep. Therefore ranchers are no longer their enemies—indeed, the few who run breeding herds of horses, regularly rounded up and branded, in the high hills like to see some feral donkeys around, for a curious reason. The only surviving wild predator there capable of preying on the horse is the puma or mountain lion, which attacks wild mustangs and tame brood mares (but especially foals) alike. Even the adult horse is no match for the puma, but the wild donkey will see him off, and donkey foals seldom fall victim to him. The occasional wild-bred mule is not afraid of pumas either, and this is perhaps the reason why the venerable mule-mare mentioned in Chapter 4 above was elected leader of a herd of wild horses.

The natural enemies of the mountain burro are therefore two. The Game Departments of the states concerned, which obtain their revenue by the sale of game licences, and have to use these funds to restock their territory with big-horn sheep and mountain goats when numbers of these are depleted, are as touchy about competitive grazing as ranchers on the plains ever were. The second enemy is the 'mustanger' in the employ of or contracting with the dog-food canners. Now, the legal status of the mustang and the burro is anomalous. It belongs to no man if it is not running on private land, and a vast area of the Rocky Mountains is in public ownership, though much of it is leased to graziers by the Federal Government. Neither the mustang nor the burro are game, or 'wild life', as legally defined, since neither were part of the pre-Columbian fauna of America and, therefore, they are not afforded the protection of those laws, Federal or state, which ensure humane treatment (in different ways) to wild and to domestic animals. Any two-legged brute has been legally free to make what money he can, by whatever means he can, out of the burros, and they have, like the mustangs, been shamelessly exploited. The object is to get these animals (which have never been herded or handled) to abattoirs often hundreds of miles away from their habitat. There is no question of shooting and butchering on the spot. They are pursued on the ground, where the terrain permits, in jeeps, and driven between converging fences into corrals, whence those of them that have not been crushed to death (foals are often crushed flat) are driven through chutes into trucks which either drive direct to the abattoir—a long journey without food or water for already exhausted and dehydrated animals—or else transhipped into freight trains to the same end. Where jeeps cannot make their way over the rugged mountains the animals are herded from the air by helicopter, thrown into a panic by the racketing din of the machine, which 'buzzes' them repeatedly, then if they still will not turn towards the corral they are 'deflected' by shooting the leaders of the herd in one side of the neck with shotguns. Needless to say, the marksmanship cannot be guaranteed. Inspectors have found animals with shotgun wounds all over the body, often with both eyes shot out, and yet still alive, in trucks on the way to the canning factory. The International Society for the Protection of Mustangs and Burros exists for the purpose of ending this traffic. It is campaigning both in the state legislatures and in the Federal House of Representatives and the Senate for a redefinition of the legal status whereby the protection of the law is extended to these animals, as it already is to game and domestic stock. Their President, "Wild Horse Annie" (Mrs Velma Johnson of Reno, Nevada), has impressed Congressmen by the force of her evidence given to committees. The title International signifies the intention to devote similar efforts to adjacent areas of Canada and Mexico when their task at home is nearer completion. Meanwhile, since the present state of the law forbids the pursuit on private property, the Society has gained possession of a Reserve for Burros in California, extending to 3,000,000 (yes, three million!) acres. California, however, is not the only state affected. Nevada, and especially Colorado, in the Grand Canyon region, are other areas where the wild herds risk being subjected to these brutalities.

To the donkey, Africa south of the equator counts as a new world, since there no wild asinine species existed (its ecological place being filled by the zebra), and consequently no tame derivative was present in ancient times. South of the Sudan there was a slow penetration of the domestic ass, at first into Ethiopia. Somewhere inside the borders of this ancient empire the territorial dividing-line between the habitat of the Somali and Nubian races of wild ass must have run. And it is on the borders of this country, of the Sudan, and of Eritrea that the best of the very few photographs of the Nubian species in the wild were taken some thirty-five years ago by the late Mrs Michael Mason.

Its high altitudes and dry climate suit the ass to perfection, and there, in what is for Africa good grazing country, a very fine type of ass was bred from early times. This is one of the countries where transport will never become totally mechanized because of the mountainous terrain. It is also one of the few countries where the horse ranks socially low in the hierarchy of working animals. To quote a recent English traveller: "No Ethiopian gentleman would be seen riding a horse." The

proper mount for the upper classes there is a mule. This applies
even to the uppermost class—the imperial family. A great deal
of hoary Hebrew tradition has rubbed off on this ancient empire.
"Lion of Judah" is not among the styles and titles of the Negus
for nothing. Some matters of ceremony must have been transmitted in high antiquity through South Arabia to Ethiopia, by
way of the Court of the Queen of Sheba, and the fact that the
King of Kings of Ethiopia has been seen mounted on a mule
on state occasions is a living reminder of this link, and especially
of the fact that King Solomon—to whom the traditions of contact between ancient Judah and Ethiopia are traced back—was
enthroned as chosen ruler not on a chair of state but in the
mule-saddle of his father King David.

To turn from majesty to utility, the Ethiopian mule has been
the mainstay of British transport systems in many campaigns
over difficult country down to quite recent times. This was so
not only in the war of liberation which the Emperor waged
against the Italians as our ally, at a time when we were desper-
ately short of allies able effectively to fight on land alongside
our armies, but subsequently in the Italian and Burmese campaigns, when many pack transport units in the mountains and
the jungles used Ethiopian mules. In Ethiopia itself, however,
the mule is primarily a riding animal, while the donkey carries
the pack. The title *In Ethiopia with a Mule* suggests a Victorian
memoir; but it is not. It is the title of a book published in 1968,
written by Dervla Murphy about a journey she made in the
1960s.

Because, before the European penetration of Africa, the
horse was not seen south of the Ethiopian border, the mule was
also absent. So from this point the donkey went it alone, on a
progress that can hardly be traced in terms of centuries, since
the criteria for dating are almost entirely lacking. But without
any sort of outside interference the donkey filtered down, under
entirely African auspices, in the remote past as far as Kenya,
where Masai herdsmen used it, and perhaps still use it, to transport their goods and chattels in the wake of the wandering
herds of cattle. There, just short of the equator, the Pilgrimage
of the Ass ceased for many centuries. Though for thousands of
years tribe after tribe has migrated down the east coast of
Africa towards the Cape, none of them brought asses with

them. The Hottentots were among the earliest to come down
into South Africa, and they brought with them only cattle.
Various Bantu tribes, such as the Matabele and Zulu, were still
coming into the country when the first European settlement
was made, and they brought with them only cattle.

So there were no asses in southern Africa until the arrival of
the Dutch in 1652. In addition to horses (brought from Java,
of all places) the Dutch brought asses from home in 1689 and
they increased and multiplied. Climatically, it was for them an
enormous change for the better. Low-lying, cold, and damp,
the Netherlands are near to the limits of tolerable habitation
by asinine standards. The climate of South Africa, on the other
hand, with its dry, clear air and grateful warmth, is just what
the donkey thrives on, and the transplanted stock grew far
beyond the stunted North European stature. That is, if all the
imports came from the Netherlands, which seems open to
doubt. The settlement which took place under Dutch auspices
did not consist of Dutch people entirely. Good old Afrikaner
names like Villiers and Marais remind us that there was a strong
Huguenot element from the first. Now, these Protestants came
predominantly from the Midi, or at any rate not farther north
than La Rochelle, and they would have the means of procuring
fine, upstanding Mediterranean-type asses. Moreover, these
were the people who founded the Cape vineyards. We have
seen throughout this story how the donkey has followed the
vintner down the years and across the continents. Was not
history repeating itself here also? If the donkeys did not draw
the long Voortrekker wagons they drew the equally famous
Cape Carts, over the Drakensberg mountains and any other
mountains they came across, and down to the Vaal and the
Orange River. For South Africa is the country where the ass
is more prominent in harness than anywhere else in the world,
and proportionately fewer donkeys went under the pack-saddle.
One sees in old saddlers' catalogues destined for the export
trade specifications and sketches for ass-harness in sets for a
team of up to sixteen animals, meant for South African custo-
mers.

The South African likes in his sports to recreate frontier
conditions. A South African gymkhana is quite unlike the
English version—mounted games for pony-club children. It is

much more an affair of grown men in such events as tent-pegging, beheading a dummy 'Turk' with a sabre, shooting balloons with a pistol, from the saddle at speed. Any big agricultural show in South Africa has on its programme driving events consisting of races with stripped-down versions of the pioneering 'long-wagon', drawn sometimes by teams of black Friesian horses but sometimes by teams of magnificent draught mules, also black. Mules were first bred in South Africa for military purposes during the Napoleonic wars, and the industry continued into this century, fluctuating as the military demand fluctuated.

A cousin of mine now resident in Natal but brought up in Zululand tells me that donkeys were brought into Zululand, and extensively bred there after the rinderpest epidemic of 1897. This plague made a clean sweep of cattle in that province, and before the stock had been built up again it was decimated by another epidemic ailment called East Coast Fever. In the early years of this century the ass had replaced the ox in the Zululand wagon team. He says, "We found the donkeys extremely hardy little animals, not only for their immunity to disease but for their ability to thrive on a countryside which appeared to have hardly any grass or herbs." But, of course, by contrast with some landscapes in which the ass, wild or tame, had been forced to pick up a living, Zululand was a land flowing with milk and honey. "Donkeys", he continues, "were very cheap, also. There was a time when they could be bought for a few shillings each." He ends with a reminiscence of his boyhood in Zululand during the First World War, of himself and his brother going off to a boarding-school and coming back home from the nearest station (fifty-four miles) regularly by donkey-wagon.

South Africa is the nearest land to Tristan da Cunha; and not very near at that. In this remote volcanic island perhaps the strangest interlude in the history of the ass was played out. In the patriarchal society of Tristan da Cunha before the eruption and evacuation, donkeys were kept by leading citizens purely for prestige purposes. They did practically no work. There were carts on the island, but these were entirely drawn by oxen. Mere possession of a donkey gave one status, and never mind the utility. I think the reason for this is that the founder of the colony, and ancestor of the majority of its inhabitants

today, Corporal William Glass, Royal Artillery, had done most
of his service as a mule-driver in an artillery ammunition
column when stationed at the Cape. Proof of the donkey's
valour arose out of the period when the island was for a time
uninhabited by the Sons of Glass. When the volcano blew up
and the rescue party came to take off the islanders they were
advised to turn all their grazing stock loose, for there was
plenty of natural water for them, and grass grows all the year
round, but either to take their dogs with them or destroy them.
The former was done, but not the latter. When in the fullness
of time some Tristanians came back to their isle the dogs had
considerably altered the balance of grazing stock on the island.
There were no sheep now, and fewer cattle. No calves. But the
number of adult donkeys was the same, and there were several
donkey foals. Which proves that the jack that can stand off the
puma of the Rockies is also a match for *Canis feralis trista-
nensis.*

New Zealand is about the only country in the Southern
Hemisphere where the donkey has never been a significant
element in the acclimatized European livestock. Probably because the climate makes it so easy to keep horses that a cheap, and
hardier or more frugally living, substitute was never necessary.
Australia is another matter. Apart from the utter desolation of
its dead and desiccated heart, the acreage that ranges in
humidity from rather dry to arid greatly exceeds that which
has a moderate rainfall. Donkey country. Also a mining country.
Just as in the American West the small prospector loaded his
gear onto a donkey and set off in search of the precious metal
on foot, so too in Australia. But there was also up to the 1930s
a very considerable number of Australian asses and mules working in harness. Their numbers in the drier regions would have
been greater had not the Australians, alone among European
'colonials', had the idea of introducing the Bactrian camel from
Afghanistan, and using it extensively for dry-country transport,
both pack and draught. Otherwise still more asses and mules
would have been needed. The numbers still in work today are
very small indeed, but the numbers running wild have not been
counted. But figures as high as ten thousand feral donkeys on
one station (admittedly an Australian cattle station covers a
big area) have been mentioned. These run mostly in the same

sort of country as brumbies. Brumbies are the Australian equivalent of the mustang—they have not so much been turned loose in the first instance as escaped owing to the negligence of the owners. They are the descendants of strays rather than of cast-offs, as is the case with the ass. As is the mustanger in the Rocky Mountain states, so has always been the brumby-hunter in Australia, only his object is that of the earlier generation of mustangers: extermination, not exploitation. As no possible financial return can come from disposal of the carcasses, the aim is to destroy the animals as cheaply as possible, and somehow dispense with the labour of burying or cremating them. Even the cost of cartridges is grudged, and this has led to the most revolting barbarities which I do not wish to describe here in detail; suffice it to say that poison is the least atrocious of the means employed. None of these means are outlawed. Some are practised by Government agents. Australian law is ruthless when it comes to pest-destruction, because of bitter experience in the past. In no overseas country have there been so many ill-advised attempts to introduce European fauna, with such fatal results. Literally scores of species have been brought in by 'acclimatizers', and almost all have proved intolerable pests to the stockman. All this recoils on the innocent head of the runaway Australian ass.

7 The Donkey in Today's World

THE white Damascus Ass, the donkey de luxe, with its large stature, easy paces, and high speed, though long a feature of upper-class town life in the Near East, was probably not originally bred by the townsmen but by desert-dwellers who had

Donkey with traditional Antrim pattern of pack-saddle and woven rush numnah. Originally designed for ponies
[*Ulster Folk Museum*

no other material possessions or products of value. The characteristic light colour, and relatively fast pace, give rise to the conjecture that this may be the one instance in which in the distant past the domestic ass of African origin has been crossed with Asiatic onagers. The obvious period for this to have taken place is that remote one in which the onager was itself a domestic animal. The cross has been proved, by experiment in modern zoos, to produce fertile progeny of either sex.

But what is more remarkable is that the cross of wild blood has been reintroduced periodically right down to this century. A contributor to the *International Standard Bible Encyclopaedia* wrote, in 1930, "the Sulaib Arabs of the Syrian desert who have no horses have a famous breed of swift and hardy grey asses, which they assert they cross at intervals with the wild asses of the desert".

In other words, these people retained right down to our own day the technique of the primeval stock-breeder which was applied to all large grazing animals. The control of adult bulls or stallions was quite simply beyond them. They therefore tethered their cow or mare on the outskirts of their settlement as soon as she came in season and lay in wait to see that the wild bull or wild stallion came out of the wilderness to cover

Donkey carrying peat in wicker panniers, Co. Fermanagh, 1924
[*Ulster Folk Museum*

her. There are ancient pictures of this happening on the rocks of Ferghana, in Persia, where according to tradition the "Heavenly Horses" were got out of tame mares by wild stallions that came 'out of the mountains' but were never caught. This is also a tenable interpretation of the rock-drawing of a tethered (if not snared) ass guarded by bowmen at Wadi Abu Wasil, in Upper Egypt.

Doughty wrote about tribes such as the Sulaib, who in his day existed in the Central Arabian desert, as being unlike other Bedouin in having no horses or camels, and very little livestock other than their asses. They were renowned for their skill in tracking small game. Since his day modernization has made life ever harder for people living at this—sub-Bedouin—level, and probably the last of them has by now been forced into some kind of sedentary existence, after thousands of years of survival in such inhospitable tracts of desert as would support no other human life.[1] But if the refreshment of their donkey-stock did depend on the services of the wild stallions, then life will have become impossible anyway with the disappearance of the Syrian onager, which like the ostrich and the oryx has vanished from the desert in our lifetime, hunted to extinction by officers and gentlemen in the armed forces of various Arab states, mounted in jeeps and armed with sub-machine guns, blazing away regardless at everything that moves.

The 'white' riding-ass, now widely distributed throughout the Middle and Near East, and called here for brevity the Damascus Ass, was first bred in Syria, which lies on the borders of that territory in which the Asiatic Wild Ass or onager was once kept and (we presume) bred for draught purposes. It is faster than any other breed of domestic ass, and there is reason to think that, as between wild species, the Asiatic wild asses or onagers were faster than the African varieties. Xenophon said of the Persians of Cyrus's day that even on their best horses they could not run down the onager: whereas Arrian, a later cavalry general, and an admirer of Xenophon's writings, says that hunters on Libyan horses were able to catch the African wild ass. We have no reason to believe that the Libyan horses

---

[1] According to the late Carl Raswan in *The Black Tents of Arabia* (Hutchinson, 1935) the Sulaib were still making a living off the desert, mainly by hunting, and still donkey-borne, about 1934.

were faster than the Persian—rather the contrary. Moreover, there are Roman pictures in north-west Africa of hunters on horseback in pursuit of the local variety of wild ass—now extinct, but plentiful in the Atlas region in Roman times. Romans were not the sort of people to go hunting something they knew they could not catch. A cross, therefore, between the African and the Asiatic species would in all probability be faster than the former, though slower than the latter. Colour variations such as white (really a pale grey, and not the albino freak, which shows a total deficiency of pigmentation) might very well occur in a hybrid between two races, neither of which produced white individuals if pure-bred. And if no fresh onager blood had been introduced into the White Ass stock since, say, 2000 B.C., it would not be surprising that the breed shows so few external characteristics of the onager, as opposed to those of the true asses. (And, of course, in Egypt, and in urban areas of the Levant, the wild cross is not possible.) Since experimentation proves the progeny of the onager/African cross to be fertile in both sexes, a mingling of the two species could have been realized very quickly.

Prizewinners including white 'Egyptian' (more likely Syrian)
ass, Islington Show, one hundred years ago
[*Illustrated London News*

Very few specimens of this strain have been brought back from the Orient to England, but the giant white 'Egyptian' Jack exhibited by the Prince of Wales, which won third prize at Islington Donkey Show in 1866, was certainly one of these, and twenty years later another super-ass from the same source was to be seen ridden in Battle and Hastings by none other than the Duchess of Cleveland, then occupant of Battle Abbey. This animal was about fourteen hands high; when it carried the Duchess it had a side-saddle, with snaffle bridle, but the manner in which Her Grace is seen in extant photographs, wielding the stick in the traditional Levantine manner, suggests that probably the bridle was more for decoration than for steering, and that direction was indicated as of old, by taps on the side of the neck. The latter ass was undoubtedly either descended from or included among those brought home by Lord Kitchener from Egypt (or according to another account from Palestine, which is equally possible), and presented to the Royal Family. The Duchess had been a bridesmaid at the wedding of Queen Victoria. The photograph we have dates from 1896.

Such direct progress from the Near East to the British Isles has been rare in the extreme, and the typical British donkey with its rather dark grey colouring and small size is the descendant of many generations that have moved by slow stages (some of them lasting hundreds of years) from various points on the north shore of the Mediterranean, the actual immigrant generation having crossed over from France, less often from Spain. I leave out of account recent arrivals from Ireland, since all but a handful of these, ancestrally speaking, will have been re-immigrants, their forebears having first reached Ireland from here.

They were not brought here primarily for riding purposes, though probably all of them were ridden one way or another, quite incidentally, by some driver 'returning empty', or even sitting on top of or behind his load, as was not uncommon also in the case of pack-horse drivers. Donkeys in harness were also somewhat uncommon here until the nineteenth century. Most of the time they worked under the pack-saddle, nearly always at odd jobs in minor trades. The only major industry with which they seem to have had some links was mining.

Donkeys, so far as I can discover, never worked underground

in any English pit, but they worked on the surface at many coal-mines in the North of England. Durham is the typical English mining county, and significantly the 'cuddy', as the ass is called north of the Tees, has a large place in the folklore of Geordieland. Even its national anthem, *The Blaydon Races*, has that beautiful and melodious line

Cried oot, 'Wheea staal the cuddy?'

Our picture of a pithead from the Walker Gallery, Liverpool,

Victorian chimney sweep out hunting

by an unknown hand, and only tentatively dated 'late eighteenth century', shows a Northern coal-pit at a time when ability to win the mineral really out-stripped the means of getting it away. There was a quite 'modern' pump and lift both operated by the same static steam-engine, but no railway to take the coal away. It had to be carted to the nearest navigable water (usually by this time a canal). Here are the carts of the typical County

With or without class-conscious funny captions, this did sometimes happen

Durham 'coup' pattern, and side by side with them the cuddy, equipped with panniers. The pannier loads are only for the short haul, however; the coal they carried will be used to stoke the furnace of the steam winding-engine. (P. 107)

Donkeys were also used for local delivery of coal in small lots direct from the pithead, mostly among the small, family-operated mines that ceased to be worked in North Yorkshire about a hundred years ago, in what are now peaceful and totally un-industrial valleys like Rosedale, Farndale, and Glaisdale. In such businesses the men worked in the pit (as well as running a smallholding and keeping a flock of sheep on the moor) and the women delivered the output, measured by the chaldron of 84 pound, by donkey. Two chaldron was one ass-load. Hard graft for one and all.

But also in parts of the North donkeys were regularly ridden by the miners to and from work. As often as not pit-heads were sited far from the nearest inhabited place, and before the hideous pit-villages were built the men often had to cross miles of lonely moor from their homes. Such was the case, for instance, with the lead-mines on Greenhow Hill above Wharfedale, and at one time each of the miners there had his donkey which he used to ride to the pit-head, turn loose on the open moor, and pick up again when his shift was over.

Otherwise the donkey was the servant of small trades, mostly concerned with cleaning of one kind or another. A German visitor to London in the reign of James I took the laundryman's donkey to be so typical of the metropolitan scene that he has left us a lifelike sketch of it, carrying washing and laundryman and all, in his illustrated album dated 1625. The chimney-sweep down to Victorian times traditionally carried his brushes and bags of soot on donkey-back (exceptionally in a little ass-cart); and we all remember the grim Mr Grimes in Kingsley's *Water Babies*, and his donkey.

Scavenging of all kinds has ever been the English donkey's lot, and even now the lords and ladies of the equine world still in some parts have their paddocks cleaned up daily with the aid of a donkey and cart. One wonders how many of the asses that act as tranquillizing travelling companion to race-horses also double the part of sanitary orderly when not engaged at race-meetings.

When I was a child in a small coastal resort in the North-east the most senior employees of our local council were two old men and a donkey, who between them operated a miniature dust-cart. They did not empty the bins behind the houses, but patrolled the streets, front and back, sweeping up casual rubbish and carting it away. (Our streets were on a proper Victorian plan; every street had its corresponding back street.) Victorian traditions and tempo of life lingered in provincial England a long time after Kaiser Wilhelm's war, and I think this trio represented the last of the Victorian crossing-sweeper tradition. What the sweeper swept off his crossing was not so much mud—which in towns became a thing of the past quite early in the nineteenth century—but horse manure, of which ever larger quantities were being deposited, urbanly as well as rurally, to the annoyance of District Councils, right up to the time when the motor-car really began to get a hold on provincial England. So the old boys and their moke were still doing a fair amount of business right through the nineteen-twenties,

Municipal scavenger donkey, c. 1925
[*Saltburn Urban District Council*

and in a sense they represented the lesser fleas which great
fleas had on their backs to bite 'em: because the last really
coprogenic horses to ply our streets, surviving the ice-cream
float and the pony-drawn milk-cart and the fish-trolleys (driven
by blue-bonneted ladies from the neighbouring fishing villages
at a furious pace, to the accompaniment of eldritch shrieks of
'Erreen, fresh 'erreen-a-a-a' or 'Feesh, feesh feeeesh!') by many
years, were the mountainous Clydesdale geldings—also the
property of the Health Department—which emptied the bins
of household refuse.

Some of the old chaps' business was very much on the side.
It was notorious that they kept compostable matter quite separate from their other sweepings; and rather than make the long
trek out to the municipal rubbish-dump they were only too
willing to oblige keen horticulturists for a consideration, with a
little cartload of the best fertilizer for roses or rhubarb. This
closely knit and long-lived team were typical of the odd-job
employment that was the donkey's lot in Victorian England.

That was at the seaside. People often wonder how donkeys
spend the off-season, the nine months or so of the typical
English year when there is no pleasure-beach business going.
Part of the answer is that the coastwise donkey, as an English
institution, is older than the seaside resort, which does not date
back before the days of George III at the earliest. Farmers, and
not only small farmers, near the sea have been in the habit of
keeping donkeys for many centuries, largely for jobs that
entailed going up and down to the beach. In the days before
chemical dressings this was important. Whereas inland farmers
dressed their fields with chalk or marl, those in coastal districts
used sand (to lighten heavy clays), seaweed as organic manure,
and sea-shells for alkali. Donkeys were the ideal means of getting these natural dressings and fertilizers up from the beach,
often in places where no road led down to the shore. The season
for doing this was short. For instance, in the parts of Devon where
the practice was common sea-ware was only gathered and
spread in the months of February and March, but it was worth
while keeping the donkeys idly at grass (well, not so much grass
as furze and thistles) all the rest of the year, purely on account
of the service they rendered during those two months. When
holidays at the seaside became a regular custom of the middle-

class townsman the donkeys were standing around doing nothing during the summer, so that any work they did by way of taking holiday-making children and adults for rides was sheer gain to the owner.

The streets of fishing-villages and small seaports are often narrow and steep, being virtually built up the side of a cliff. Clovelly with its stair-climbing donkeys is the obvious West-country instance, but there are scores if not hundreds of Clovellys round our shores.

Narrowly built itself, the donkey is admirably adapted for traffic in narrow alleys (that is why it was in such demand in the towns of the Near East), and its climbing powers are re-nowned. There are no streets narrower, or steeper (indeed some of them are more like ladders down the cliff), than those that lead down to the Esk in the ancient port of Whitby, a mere hour's donkey-walk from the desk at which I write. Some ninety years ago, when the great days of the Whitby whaling trade were a living memory still, and its North Sea herring fishery was booming, the milk float and pony were unknown in the town. All milk was delivered from donkeys, and fortunately for amateurs of the ass, it was delivered to Frank Sutcliffe, among others, one of the most gifted, and earliest, of English photo-graphers. His glass negatives are still in good shape, and they show us the milk-round of the 1880s, with a can seemingly of about eight-gallon capacity, but unlike any milk-can now or recently in use, slung either side of a pack-saddle on a donkey. These cans—and so far as one can see the type of saddle— are identical with those shown on the Harrogate milk-round of an earlier generation, in the illustrations to Walker's *Costume of Yorkshire* (1804). The only difference seems to be in the get-up of the donkey. As was only to be expected in a fashion-able spa like Harrogate, the dairy moke there was elaborately turned out and clipped, and it was *de rigueur* to clip round the tail in rings all the way down, giving a curious saw-edged effect.

At that period the London costermonger would not have been complete without his moke and barrow, the latter being almost identical in design with the Irish general-purpose ass-cart. In the year of the Great Exhibition, 1851, Henry Mayhew reported in *London Labour and the London Poor* that on Saturday mornings "the costers' business day, as many as two

thousand donkey-barrows visit this market [Covent Garden]".
They came principally from the East End and South London.
From the thirties to the sixties of this century my daily work
was done within sight, within earshot, and most pungently of
all within smelling distance of Mud Salad Market. By the time
of the Festival of Britain, 1951, there was not a donkey to be
seen in the Market, though horse-drawn carts still lingered on
there for a few more years.

London coster with donkey barrow, *c.* 1851

Milk-round at Whitby, late 1870s
[*Photo Frank Sutcliffe*

Little by little the workaday employment of the donkey in Britain withered away. Perhaps it was artificially prolonged into the middle forties by petrol-rationing and suchlike shortages (but not nearly so much in Britain as in Ireland). Certainly by the early sixties the asinine population of the country had fallen lower than it had been for about a thousand years.

An estimate made on the eve of the Second World War gave the number of donkeys in Britain as less than a hundred all told, and at that time the London Zoo could not find a single entire jack in the whole country. I am inclined to think this was a case of not looking hard enough. There are at the present time half-a-dozen 'beach' donkeys at the seaside town only four miles from where this book is being written, and they are not a revival. They have been present in about the same numbers since late Victorian times, according to local testimony. Now, there are six resorts of about the same size, similarly equipped, on the coast of Yorkshire, and about as many comparable *plages* in Durham and Northumberland, with similar histories. For such a group of seasonally working donkeys one can reckon one or two others not on public view—jacks unsuitable for riding, jennies with small foals at foot, for instance. That would give a probable total, for the period in question, of more than seventy-two between the Humber and the Tweed alone. The ass in Britain leads an underground existence statistically, because it is and has been beneath the notice of the Ministry of Agriculture, which alone takes livestock censuses.

An impenetrable fog also surrounds the occurrence of the mule in Britain in recent times. Some ninety years ago an impeccable local historian wrote, "Within the last thirty-five years [*i.e.*, since about 1847] I have seen hundreds of tons of coal brought into [the Esk valley] in three-hundredweight long sacks, on packhorses *and mules.*" Now, Canon Atkinson's material is all what intelligence organizations used to classify as A1; not only was the informant of proved and consistent

Loading the milk donkey, late 1870s
[*Photo Frank Sutcliffe*

veracity, but the information he provided was of its nature inherently probable. And yet I can find no other written source of the same period which confirms this employment of mules in our countryside; and among the many museums in the North Riding which have collections of rural bygones there are none which possess any items of pack-gear characteristic of the mule's equipment.

The same might indeed be said of earlier periods. For instance, a contemporary picture of the English army advancing to the battle of Flodden shows clearly in its supply train a number of mules, and possibly some asses also. But among detailed contemporary accounts of the battle there is no mention of mules (though there is of 'sumpter' horses); we have a list of several hundred receipts for horses returned to farmers after the Flodden campaign for which they had been requisitioned, but none for mules. Yet that is not to say that because no supporting evidence survives, either Canon Atkinson or the unknown war-artist of 1513 was wrong!

And then the donkey benefited, late in the day, by a curious revulsion of feeling engendered by the Machine Age. The first beneficiary of this emotional backwash was the horse. People whose whole war had been spent in mechanized units, people whose weekday work began and ended with an ever-repeated journey by car and bus and train to factory or office, people who saw themselves fated for ever to pursue some indoor avocation, and to spend their whole lives dealing with words and figures instead of people and animals, turned to horses and riding in their leisure hours as an antidote to bricks and mortar and petrol, and as the means of a mental gear-change, down to the steadier tempo of an earlier age, as a means perhaps to solitude, that commodity that has become increasingly rare in overcrowded Western Europe throughout the lifetime of my age-group. Certainly to many the horse was a link, often unconsciously sought, with a simpler world of earth and grass and sky, where wind and weather, rain and sunshine, were the ultimate realities as of olden time.

For twenty post-war years this movement, which had been evident enough before the outbreak of Hitler's War, gained momentum. In the middle sixties it began to spill over into neighbouring countries in a manner reminiscent of the Anglomania which swept the Continental upper classes in the years just before the invention of the railway. Years when the English mail-coach and the English racehorse meant Speed absolutely. Years when the imitation Corinthian or imitation Meltonian in every country from Sweden to Spain was 'fast' in every sense of the word. And now the world was glutted with speed. The sort of English week-end life, spent among horses, was not envied by Europeans because of its speed but because of its leisurely pace, and the English equines that began to be fashionable were not the largest or the fastest, but ponies and cobs on which to potter about. All the signs are that though this renewed passion for the horse has yet a long and mounting course to be run on the Continent, in Britain it has reached its peak, and may be on the verge of a decline.

The reason is that leisure spent with horses does not automatically imply a release from the rat-race, still less a refuge into which one can withdraw temporarily at will. If you are committed to the horse (and it is fatally easy to become so committed), then you are in up to the neck all the time. Nor

Harrogate milk boy, *c.* 1800
[From G. Walker, *Costume of Yorkshire*

will it deliver you from the bondage of the internal combustion engine. Far from it. To the works sedan and the family saloon is added the one-pony or two-horse trailer, and inevitably, sooner or later, the Land-Rover, and perhaps ultimately the horse-box. There is a coming and going of motorized hay-wagons, of feed-merchants' lorries. There is the eternal and increasingly less successful quest for near-by paddocks for exercise and grazing, leading to a change of domicile to where these are more attainable, if not actually part of the property. And the whole thing is horribly and increasingly expensive. The price of everything connected with the horse has risen steeply ever since 1945—but not the price of horses themselves, which means that those who sought to pay for their riding by a little breeding of foals found themselves committed to even heavier investment with negligible returns.

For these and similar reasons the ass, which had once filled a very backstairs niche in the prosperous Country House establishment of the Victorians, returned after more than half a century to the more modest country homes (without any capital letters) of the neo-Elizabethans. Whereas of yore it had pulled the lawn-mower and been tended (if that is the word) by the gardener's boy, it now receives the daily attention of the lady of the house, for there is no gardener's boy, and no gardener either, unless the master of the house be himself horticulturally inclined. Whereas in days of yore it carried the toddling children of the house in a kind of wickerwork howdah, escorted by an ambling, clucking Nanny, there is no Nanny now; at best a Portuguese *au pair*; and the same Lady of the House, doubling yet another part, is not available to amble alongside, for she is herself leading the donkey. In the whole set-up, the donkey is the only one who is not in some sort of reduced circumstances. How mightily, on the contrary, is its status increased!

For a few years in the mid-Victorian era there had been a Donkey Show, in the impressive surroundings of the Agricultural Hall, Islington, but it fell into desuetude and was not replaced by anything else; neither were there classes for donkeys at agricultural shows—not even at that kind of exhibition, still not extinct in the North Country, which begins with a class for Cleveland Bay Brood Mares and ends with one for Six Brown Eggs or a Plate of Ginger Parkin. The Royal Show ceased to have a place for donkeys after 1904, and the International Horse Show (Olympia) after 1914.

Now arose the Donkey Show Society founded in 1967, since when it has already changed its name to the Donkey Breed Society, as being more appropriate to its avowed main object, the improvement of the quality of donkeys kept in Britain. To which end showing is only a means. Bitter experience with horses has demonstrated to many of its members how easily that means can supplant the end. The same applies to dogs, too, for that matter. There seems to be a fatal sort of gravitation whereby the race which is bred to excel at shows becomes in the end fit for nothing else but the show arena. In particular, competitive showing is not calculated to improve temperament. This activity resembles war, not only in the fact that the people who organize both of them are great patrons of eyewash, God's gift to the manufacturers of pipeclay and metal polish. But for the exhibitor and for the exhibited, if not for the spectator, the show-ring, like the battlefield, affords long periods of intensely boring waiting, alternating with short periods of extreme anxiety. Neither is good for the temper of man or beast.

The official foundation of the Society was in fact the culmination of some seven years of increasing interest and more and more intensified effort by those who became its founders, and public discussion leading to its institution had gone on since 1965, by which year at least one English stud had sold some three hundred head, mostly of Irish origin.

It remains to be seen whether the desired improvement of quality is to be achieved by the re-introduction of superior breeding strains from abroad or by the amelioration of the breed 'from within' by mating only the best with the best of existing stock, as the Breed Society recommends. Perhaps 'reintroduction' in itself points to the heart of the problem. Many times in the past good stock has been imported, at least from the days of the Burton Spanish jackass in 1116. However, generations of life in the chilly damp of a British winter outdoors have produced the characteristic dwarfing, accompanied by a head disproportionate in size to the body and limbs, which tends to overtake any species native to a hot, dry climate when it migrates to a cold, humid one.

Some importations with a view to upgrading by outcrossing

have already taken place. But in the long run the effect of these infusions of blood will not be so great as the improvement effected by correct feeding and protection from the weather, in particular from rain, from fog, and from moisture-laden winds. Nature affords very little protection. The donkey in the latitude of the fifties grows a coat that one would think might defy the onslaught of all the soaking Atlantic gales that blow over the British Isles.

And one would be wrong. The long coat is indeed a response to the challenge of the environment, but an unavailing one. The long coat of the North-western donkey is not weatherproof in the sense that the coats of Exmoor, Shetland, or Highland ponies are weatherproof. There is, for instance, no 'double pile' of inner and outer hairs such as the Exmoor grows. Something perhaps in the texture of the individual hairs, but more probably in the way they are arranged, invalidates them as a raincoat. The 'lie of the hair' in equines is their first line of protection against cold and damp. Individual hairs are so parted, and their tips point in such a way, as to drain the water off from the back without running down the sides and under the belly, in all pony breeds long domiciled in a wet climate. More important, they have developed a thick tuft of hair at the very root of the tail, which prevents water running down between the hind-legs. This the ass totally lacks.

It would seem as if by growing this would-be waterproof coat the ass has expended vital forces which in the race as a whole would have served to let it grow to the stature of its Mediterranean ancestors. I am reliably informed this explanation is not biologically tenable, and must bow to the opinion of the learned. Nevertheless, the equation—the smaller the shaggier—remains generally true of these latitudes, and it is up to the scientist to explain it by some other means. Some kind of proof by observation could be managed by recording the coat-length of successive generations of Sicilian or Ceylonese dwarf donkeys resettled in the North Temperate Zone. These cannot in practice become much smaller than they are already, one would think. If they do over the generations grow longer coats, and stay at their present size, you may enter the author—posthumously, perhaps—in the appropriate class at the Donkey Breed Society's show.

There seems to be only one exception to this ruthless rule. The giant *baudet de Poitou* is not only the biggest ass in the world but it is also the hairiest, transmitting its shagginess also to its mule offspring (judges of the Poitevin mule will reject a smooth-coated one). By what means the men of Poitou have managed to cheat nature to this extent is a mystery known only within the Department of Deux Sèvres.

So far no British breeder has taken a leaf out of the Arab Horse enthusiast's book, by importing breeding-stock from the classic lands of origin, either North Africa or Western Asia, or from those South European countries where the ass is still taken seriously. So far, such imports have been made only from Bulgaria, which though not a Mediterranean country partly enjoys what the weathermen call a Mediterranean climate, and which does not lie far off the historic route by which the ass entered in the distant past, at the dawn of the wine-drinking, olive-eating 'classical' civilization. Bulgaria is also a wine-growing country. It will be interesting to see how the Bulgar ass and its descendants respond to the changed environment.

For the first time in this country, a Donkey Stud Book has been established, and the standards laid down require the conformation to be that of a riding animal. Anatomically, this implies principally two requirements. The 'elbow' must be free— *i.e.*, not 'tied-in' to the wall of body—and this is combined with a 'laid-back' shoulder to allow the fullest possible forward movement of the limbs at every stride. So far so good—there is nothing in this incompatible with the structure of the ass as seen in the best wild specimens of all races. The second requirement is the right kind of back. This must be neither too long nor too short. There must be 'room for a saddle', and not too much spare room behind it. Once upon a time it made sense to have the longest possible back, in the days of pack traffic, when it was economic to breed an animal that would accommodate the longest possible packload (this is a factor that has conditioned various British native pony breeds, and some Mediterranean breeds of donkey). But the Donkey Breed Society is not set on breeding a pack-ass. According to the verdict passed by many judges in the English show-ring, the back should be so shaped that the saddle will stay put: in other words, it must be so naturally hollow (as in the horse) that the saddle will remain firm with a girth only, dispensing with the aid of crupper and breastplate. Now, in terms of the horse, this is entirely in harmony with the natural conformation of the animal. Look at any of the prehistoric wall-paintings of horses in the caves of France or Spain, executed by hunters of the Old Stone Age, thousands of years before the horse was domesticated. In the majority of them you will see horses on which the urge to clap a saddle is natural—the very sight of which, perhaps, awoke the invention of the saddle in the human mind. The 'top line' or undulation of the back between the wither and the hip is the same on the horse in the cavern of Les Combarelles as on the finest show-hack today.

Not so with the donkey. Its top line in Nature is one horizontal plane, and this fact is acknowledged and given due weight in R. S. Summerhays' *Points and Type of the Donkey*. Now, it may be argued that the story of human progress and the build-up of our human culture is one long flying in the face of nature, and this is where we have to fly in this matter, so modifying the anatomy of the donkey that its skeletal structure will accommodate itself to a man-made invention, and one, moreover, that was designed for use on another animal. It seems to me that the way here is to overcome Nature by some sort of detour (and the way to do this has already been demonstrated in the distant past) rather than to try to twist the asinine anatomy to suit our aims.

There are basically only two designs of saddle in the world. There is the riding saddle, which consists essentially of two arches joined by lateral bars; it was invented in Mongolia quite some time ago now, and used in conjunction with felt pads either side of the spine, of which we have ancient examples from Western Siberia. In both these lands at the time of the invention there were only horses, not donkeys. There is also the pack saddle, invented probably in North Africa, and intended from the first to fit the flat asinine back. It is basically a wooden structure, not built up of arches or forks, but more like a barrel cut laterally in half, the interior padded. From this Afro-Asian pack-saddle a side-saddle, for use on the horse, was basically derived, and was in use for many centuries. It proved highly inefficient, and was replaced in comparatively recent times by the modern side-saddle, which is a modification of the Central Asian riding saddle, *right for a horse*.

If the breeder tries to modify the conformation of the ass to suit his idea of a saddle he will probably succeed in the short run. But as stated above, you cannot have it both ways. In producing his hollow-backed ass he will set some kind of compensatory train of evolutionary events in motion, and some other physical property will be produced as a side-effect, the nature of which is unpredictable, but may well be unpleasant. What is required is a new conception of the riding-saddle based on specifically asinine requirements, having as its base not the Central Asian saddle-tree but the North African saddle-tree, as modified, for instance, in the Provençal mule-saddle. It will probably be necessary to reconcile oneself to the use of crupper and breastplate as a matter of course—but why not? These items belong traditionally to the riding equipment of asses and mules, and what was good enough for Cardinal Wolsey and the King of Aragon ought to be good enough for the modern moke-fancier. Such a saddle would probably afford the minimum contact between the rider's thighs and the animal's back and sides, but here again what is right for the horse is not necessarily right for the ass. In assmanship and mulesmanship the human voice, and gestures with the indispensable magic wand, are traditionally of more import than pressure of leg or pelvis. One does not ride a donkey 'through the seat of one's pants'.

Many members of the Donkey Breed Society are concentrating on fancy coloured strains, piebald, skewbald, and spotted, but so far there is no breakaway movement such as led to the establishment of separate horse-breeders' clubs (*e.g.*, the Spotted Horse Society, with its own stud book) based entirely on coat-colour. There seems to be no particular geographical source of coloured donkeys, either in the Old or in the New World. England, and Sussex in particular, has as good a claim as any to be the homeland of the piebald or skewbald donkey; Hastings and Battle have not only seen in their day the Duchess of Cleveland and her white Egyptian jack. In the year 1066 a certain event took place in that vicinity, vivid scenes from which are depicted in the Bayeux Tapestry, embroidered certainly before 1100, and probably in England rather than in

Normandy. Among the marginal drawings in this tapestry is one of a donkey in harness, parti-coloured.

Parti-coloured animals are usually a by-product of domestication, but it seems fancy colouring is not so much the result of domestication as such but of the fact that domestication can result in the crossing of two strains, both of wild origin, that in the wild never crossed. It may well be that parti-coloured donkeys owe their origin to the mixture in a certain proportion of the genes of two wild varieties, one of which may have been extinct for a long time; neither of the wild ancestors need necessarily have been piebald or spotted itself.

So much for the asinine revival in the British Isles. It will be followed in all probability by a similar phenomenon in Germany (where an International Donkey Register already exists), the Low Countries, and possibly Scandinavia; all countries where the past history of the ass is equally scanty, if not even scantier, than in Britain.

In France there is as yet no such movement stirring, and indeed it is not needed there so far as saving the donkey from extinction is concerned. It is true that the mule-breeding of Poitou has almost come to a standstill. But in the South, in

Provençal pack-ass today

Provence, in Roussillon, in the Pyrennean departments, there are still asses a-plenty, and mules also. They have only receded a little into the interior. In the Alpes Maritimes and the Basses Alpes you will motor a long way along the *autoroutes* without seeing either. But I saw a mule in 1969 in harness in the streets of Avignon, and though on the Riviera the ass seems to inhabit picture post-cards only, this impression was dispelled on two occasions in the following spring when I was looking for a house and land in one of the side-valleys of the Var. During the course of discussion with the notary I was required to state whether our occupation would constitute *une exploitation agricole*—if it came off. No, I said, if we keep a cow it is because we do not like your brand of tinned milk. And two stallions and an elderly brood mare do not constitute agricultural exploitation in the second half of the twentieth century. *"Mais au contraire, M. Dent,"* said my notary, *"il y a des gens par ici qui gagnent la vie avec deux chèvres, un âne ou un mulet."* The tiny cathedral city of Entrevaux is approached only by a narrow bridge across the Var, the far side of which is straddled by a gatehouse. Leading out of this is the first door in the town. On it is written the evocative phrase 'Maréchal Ferrant'. I wandered in. On the walls were narrow shoes with high caulkins of an unfamiliar pattern. I asked the farrier how he would view the prospect of adding to his clients an Arab stallion. Without perturbation, he assured me; with pleasure, even. I pointed to the wall: *"Avec des sabots comme ça?"* *"Ah, non, monsieur, ce sont des sabots de mulet. Pas pour votre étalon."* "But then," I said, "I don't see any mules here, or donkeys either." He looked at me pityingly. *"Ils sont dans la montagne. Plus loin."*

And so it was. Farther into the interior, on the departmental road to Saint-André-les-Alpes, one encountered a veritable mule of the Poitou breed, mountainous, shaggy still in early June, with legs like a four-poster bed, a broad breast, near seventeen hands high and in colouring like an Exmoor pony; it had the height and substance of a Shire horse. On the same road we saw the annual migration of the shepherd with his flocks to the mountain pastures, modified to suit the Jet Age. The flock travels up from the low country in a huge double-decker float. Before unloading the sheep the driver let down the gangway and opened a sort of postern gate. Out stepped, of his own accord and with perfect aplomb, a magnificent light-coloured ass about thirteen-and-a-half hands high, ready caparisoned with his pack saddle, on which the shepherd's complete equipment, including his blankets and a little barrel of wine, were lashed.

In Italy the donkey exists principally in Piedmont, not for its own sake but as a sire of mules, which are still used in the Alps (such mules as are still used in Switzerland are also bred in Piedmont[1]). Farther south, in the Po valley, in Etruria, Latium, and the central part of Italy generally, they are thinner on the ground than they were in 1945, owing to the progress of mechanization. But here again, in the central Apennines the donkey holds its own, and will do so as long as people are using mules to any extent. In the far South, in Calabria, Campagnia, Apulia, Lucania, and Sicily, where conditions on the whole are still more primitive than in the rest of the country, and where agricultural conditions still do not permit the tenant-farmer to go in for a tractor, both asses and

[1] And in the canton Valais

Provençal ass in harness today

mules are still used both to work on the land and for light traffic on the somewhat sketchy rural roads which exist side by side with the most advanced *autostrade*.

From one Italian region, larger than Sicily, the ass is largely and the mule entirely absent. But so they always have been. This is the island of Sardinia, the one part of Italy to possess an indigenous breed of pony which is still available, in considerable numbers, to perform all the work that is done on the mainland by mules. It is not an invariable rule that the existence of ponies about this size (thirteen hands) precludes the existence of mules; they exist, for instance, side by side in the Balkans and the Greek islands, but in most countries where it is at all common the mule is a substitute for some kind of horse (as for the harness horse, in Spain), which is therefore not represented there.

On the Greek mainland and in Albania, and in all the Greek islands, from large ones like Crete to the tiniest inhabited Ionian rock, asses and mules abound still. There are certain drawbacks about keeping motor vehicles on islands—they will perform there as well as anywhere else, but if there is a prolonged storm, causing the local steamer to miss its regular call, supplies of petrol are apt to run out. The insular ass will continue to draw its fuel from local sources, no matter how long the gale blows.

With the island of Cyprus we have already dealt in Chapter 4. The Cypriot ass is large, strong, and good-looking, and present in fair numbers. It has to be, as we implied in the previous chapter, since the famous Cypriot 'mule' is not really a mule but the offspring of a pony stallion and a jenny, so that a large donkey population has to be kept up for purposes of hybrid-breeding alone.

Another island famous in asinine history is Malta, long renowned for its strong and handsome breed of asses. It has been surmised that these asses were once identical with the Catalonian race, and were brought from Spain, but no one has hazarded a guess as to when this happened. We would agree that the two strains are probably closely related, but more likely the boot was on the other foot. Malta at one time was a base for the far-travelling Phoenician merchants, who had business also in Spain, and it seems probable that they will first have brought select Syrian asses to the island and later brought their progeny westward to the Iberian peninsula. Nothing operates more stringently, in the matter of selecting livestock, than travel by sea. It costs as much in deck-space, in labour, in space taken up by feed and water for the four-footed passenger, to ship a bad animal as a good one, and probably these mariners of Tyre and Sidon and Melita brought nothing but the best up and down their gangways. Ezekiel in his lamentation for Tyre speaks of the experience these men had in livestock transport (XXVII, 14): "They of the house of Togarmah traded in thy fairs with horses and mares and mules." Togarmah was the place in North Syria from which King Solomon got his first horses; not overland, but shipped by the mariners of his friend and ally, King Hiram of Tyre. Asses of quality are no longer bred on Malta, indeed, owing to pressure on agricultural space breeding is no longer economic. The still large asinine population of Malta is now recruited from North Africa.

The present situation of the ass is probably more favourable in Spain and Portugal than in any other Mediterranean land. Despite mechanization in the cities, the ass still has a place in the rural economy, and a good mule is prized as an animal of worth. Breeding is not haphazard, and there are still mule-raising establishments where good Andalusian mares of the more sturdy type are put to Catalonian jackasses. Moreover, in both countries the Ministries of Agriculture take an interest in the maintenance of good breeding stock. The turnout of asses and mules in the Iberian peninsula is a matter of prestige; shagginess, taken for granted in some other countries, is at a discount, and as much care is expended in clipping and trimming as in the case of horses.

It is on the south shore of the Mediterranean that the outlook, especially the long-term outlook, for the donkey appears gloomiest. For the moment there is no prospect of it becoming redundant, and the conditions under which it works are being ameliorated, both by Government action and by that of voluntary societies such as that for the Protection of Animals in North Africa and the Brooke Hospital in Cairo. The donkey in most of the Arab lands is still the poor man's horse, also his bicycle and his work-van. The discovery of oil in the first instance benefits none but the landlords who draw the royalties. The

cascade of Cadillacs that descends on the sheikly families
where oil is struck is not accompanied by a shower of minicars
for their tenants. The herdsman in the desert, the fellah in the
oasis, still have to rely on the ass, and in general according to
their abilities they do right by him. But the day will come when
some of this money—eventually a great deal of it—will filter
down to the small farmer and stock-breeder. When the landlords
became affluent, they abandoned the horse, from Morocco to
the Persian Gulf. But in this region asses are perhaps a hundred
times more numerous than horses. When the peasant gets his
minitractor, what will become of his ass? Islam forbids the
consumption of ass-meat, as of horse-meat. The redundant ass
will simply be turned on to the desert and the mountains in
his millions. And he will not stay there, the population pressure
will be too great. He will return to the cultivated lands, this
time as a predatory grazer. We have seen what happens in
Australia and the American West, where the pressure on grazing is not nearly so great. Unless timely and anticipatory
measures are taken, the inevitable mechanization of agriculture
in the Near East will be followed by unbelievable massacres of
feral asses.

One of the first side-turnings to the right taken during the
pilgrimage of the ass along the Silk Road to China thousands
of years ago was that leading south across the mountains to the
Iranian plateau. This was a land which in the distant past had
perhaps once been inhabited by wild horses, and certainly was
one of the first countries to be colonized by tame horses after
the invention of horse-breaking on the plains of Central Asia.
But while there is absolutely no trace now of the existence of
wild horses, past or present, in Persia, except for a folk tradition
of a creature called Ghur-Asb in the wilderness of Dasht-i-
Kavir, the Persian onager (Ghur-Khar), a relation of the donkey
whose acquaintance we made in the first chapter, is alive and
well in the deserts of Iran. It is strictly protected by the
country's game laws, the present stock is estimated at a thous-
and head, and what is more cheering, their numbers are increasing. Already there are more than twice as many of them as
there are of the closely related Indian Wild Ass.

During the centuries since the merchants brought the ass
south into Persia—over the same routes as the warriors had

previously driven their horses into what was then a grass country, providing very good pasturage by Middle Eastern standards—the climate has become drier and the familiar cycle of deforestation, desiccation, erosion, impoverishment, and over-grazing has run a large part of its course. The deserts have become larger and the mountains barer than ever. If cereal crops are grown they are grown by irrigation. If grazing exists it is by the grace of Allah alone, and not thanks to the operation of grass husbandry. Consequently the balance of the solid-hoof population has been reversed, and the once commoner horse has become—to quote a Teheran resident, Mrs Louise Forouz, to whom I am indebted for much information about the country —"a rare and expensive luxury". She adds that "there are probably as many breeds of asses in Iran as of horses". A white strain which seems to be identical with the prized 'Damascus' strain of white saddle asses is known here as the Bandari, and on account of its great stature (fourteen hands) costs as much to buy as a mule. This and all the better and larger types come from the South of Persia. From the South also come the smaller strains of horse. This is part of a familiar pattern whereby the local breeds of horse and ass dovetail into and are complementary to each other. The mountain ass of Persia is taller on the leg, and also stronger, with more bone, than those of the low country; while in the northern provinces, and especially on the open Turcoman steppes, they are much smaller, often as little as eight or nine hands. But the Turcoman steppe is precisely the region where a *tall* horse, called in Arab breeding circles *muniqi*, originated, and was brought down across Persia into the Arabian peninsula. Another esteemed breed of substance is the Cypriot ass (here called Quebresi). In another chapter we have noted the great qualities of the Cypriot mule (or rather, jennet), and mules are still important in Persia.

This is a country where impressive main motor roads exist, but where side roads are no more numerous or better-maintained than in the days of the Emperor Darius. Much local traffic is pack-borne, loads such as straw and firewood being often carried in bundles on the bare backs of the animals, and mules are very serviceable for this purpose. But the chief Persian users of mules are not so much farmers as the pastoral nomadic tribes of the whole country, from Kurds of the north-west to the Baluchis of the south-east, bordering on Pakistan in the provinces from which (rather than from India) the greatest nomads of all, the gipsies, originally came. All these pastoral tribes on their annual migrations from the lowlands to the mountain pastures make extensive use of the mules which they breed.

The strongest and most expensive mules are bred around Kermanshah, which from the times of Alexander the Great and earlier has been the source of big, and by Oriental standards large-boned, mares.

Except, therefore, for the far north (where the horse is still relatively common) and the mule country, the centre and the greater part of Persia is the territory of the donkey, which works in the plough and under the pack-saddle, and is ridden, both in the countryside and also in the town. In the towns they also work in harness, pulling light carts with heavy loads, along those streets which are wide enough for wheeled traffic, although as so often in the Near East, many town alleys are so narrow that local deliveries can only be made by the pack-load. Only the Caspian region of Persia is comparatively short of donkeys. This has the highest rainfall of the whole country, and is notable for a breed of pony as small as—and until recently, as cheap as—the ass. Sardinia over again.

The statistics are tantalizing in their incompleteness, but one is grateful to the Iranian Government, as being the only one in the whole region that publishes any figures at all, and the trend they show is a healthy one. There were (1961) in the whole country 2,023,427 asses and 629,936 horses and mules. One could wish this latter figure had been broken down, but as probably there are about ten asses and two mules to every horse this would probably mean that there were some 406,600 mules. The corresponding figures for 1967 are 2,500,000 asses and 433,000 mules—a reasonable rate of increase and one justified by the transport needs of the population. This is a country with main trunk roads of international standard, and no motorable country roads to speak of. This means that for many years to come the Persians will be in the position of Englishmen about a hundred years ago, when the long-distance transport was a matter for the railways. But to get the goods and passengers to and from railhead a greater number of draught animals was

required than ever before. Persia is, moreover, rather a thinly
populated country, and the state of affairs there is much
healthier than in the only other two non-Arab countries in the
Old World, where there is a considerable number of donkeys—
Pakistan and India. Both these countries not only have vast
human populations but pending huge and impossibly expensive
irrigation schemes, many of which are perfected but few completed according to schedule, while meanwhile every available acre of pasture is grossly over-grazed all the year round.
On this scanty herbage the donkey survives meagrely enough,
and his lowly status is matched by that of his owner over much
of the sub-continent. In caste-bound India, where callings are
hereditary and interlocked with the system of religious belief,
the children of a donkey-driver must also be donkey-drivers.
Their hope of improvement lies not in this world but in the
next incarnation, where if they are virtuous they may be reborn
as a member of Congress or a house-surgeon in a London hospital. And donkey-drivers rank pretty low, in the world of here
and now, in the hierarchy of caste. However, since the driver
of today might die tomorrow and be reborn 'a colt, the foal of
an ass' the day after, there is some incentive for him to treat
his charges with respect.

Ceylon, so far as the Old World donkey is concerned, is the
end of the line, and a more cheerful note on which to end this
chapter. By contrast with the Indian sub-continent, it is a fertile
island, with an equable climate. The donkeys of Ceylon are
not very numerous, but they are an arresting sight. Here the
donkey has consented to conform to the laws which govern
the rest of the animal kingdom, and specially the genus Equus,
and which decree that island races shall be or become smaller
than mainland races. It is only an occasional concession; there
are other breeds of donkey living on islands, notably Malta and
the Balearics, growing consistently to a larger size than their
Continental cousins. However, the donkey of Ceylon is a dwarf,
but a comely dwarf, of charming proportions, an attractive
dark-brown, almost coffee-colour. Some fine specimens of the
breed are kept by the Greater London Council at Battersea
and Sydenham. All donkey foals are enchanting, but Ceylonese
donkey foals especially so, with their thimble-sized hoofs and
large round eyes. If anyone had designed a plush toy, in this

shape, with this colour and texture of coat, you would say it was unreal and sentimental. But no. It seems God can be senti- mental too, sometimes.

Ceylon jenny and foal, owned and bred by Greater London Council Parks Department

[*G.L.C.*

Appendix I
Mule Train

THE American Pack Train of the United States Army is organized as follows: 1 pack-master; 1 cargador or assistant pack-master; 1 cook; 1 blacksmith; 10 packers; 1 bell-mare; 14 saddle mules; 50 pack mules. This makes the pack train comprise 14 men and 50 pack-mules and 14 saddle mules for the packers to ride. There are in the American Army, 8 of these permanent pack-trains in the United States and several in the Philippine Islands and Alaska. The number of trains in the columns varies with circumstances; oftentimes they are broken up, divided etc. as scouting, reconnoitering, etc. require. Each pack-train is supplied with the following outfit; 14 cowboy saddles, Texas pattern; 50 aparejos, complete with cruppers, canvas cinchas, saddle-blankets, coronas and sobrejalmas; 100 lair-ropes each 30 feet long, ⅜ in. dia.; 50 sling-ropes, 28 feet long, ⅜ in. dia.; 50 lash ropes, 46 feet long, ⅜ in. dia., with cincha; 10 blinds (one for every 5 mules), 100 mantas; 14 riding-bridles, curb, single rein; 14 saddle blankets, for the riding saddles; 1 picket rope, 125 ft. long, 2 in. dia.

The pack-master has immediate charge of his train of men and animals, and is responsible for the welfare of his train, its instruction and efficiency and for the equipments, etc. The Cargador acts as assistant to the pack-master and also acts as the train saddler and repairer. The packers employed with these American pack-trains should be large men, weighing from 175 lb up, and be able to lift up on the mules back and tie there a side pack equal to their own weight, 175 lb. (Nevertheless, the writer has known many medium-sized men who were expert packers in every sense of the word, practice is everything.) The importance of having large, strong, experienced men in the train soon becomes evident when their work is inquired into. On slippery mountain sides, often knee-deep in snow and slush, the pack mule must be stood sideways and the load readjusted; this required one man to stand on the down-hill side to load that side, and only tall, strong men can successfully do such work well. Oftentimes, the pack-mule, loaded, becomes mired down on the march, when it requires some of the packers to go in and get him out. This will require men used to such work and inured to it by long practice and much natural skill. It is held by the packers themselves that a strong, healthy bright man can become well acquainted with packing etc. in one month but it takes at least one year to make the new packer fairly expert and inured to his work in the train. There are two classes of packers, first and second. The first class comprises those packers that have shown the greatest expertness in all that pertains to the train service excelling in several things about the train, and only indifference in one or two other duties will debar the second-class packer from being rated a first-class packer; to gain the first class, he must excel in every individual part of his work, riding, etc., and the standard of efficiency maintained is very remarkable for its thoroughness. The pack mule in the American service must be from 4–9 years of age, either male or female, from 13½ to 16 h.h. and about 850 lb. in wt. The small blocky animal is preferred to a tall, rangy one. The pack mule should not be broken to harness, should have perfect health, especially perfect feet. . . .

It has been said in a previous chapter that the best known way to relieve the cavalry horse of the weight of his heavy pack and to carry the necessary field outfit of rations, equipments, etc. is to have a troop pack-train of mules. As these trains are old institutions in the American cavalry service, and as it may suddenly fall to the lot of the young cavalry officer to take charge of the pack-train, he should be familiar not only with methods of actual packing, but especially with the methods employed to keep the "riggings" in perfect shape and condition. Without this care, no pack-train can expect to be of continued service to the troop. Carelessness or ignorance in packing or in promptly readjusting loosened packs when on the march will do much in serious injury, but perhaps not more than neglect in fitting and shaping the rigging to the mule's back, ignorance in carefully adjusting it when in use, or carelessness in caring for the rigging when off the mule's back. Many times the troop will be called upon to traverse territory over and through which, wheeled transportation cannot pass. The illustration below shows the wheeled transportation in the American Army; the capacity etc. of these wagons is important to know in order that loads may be made up suitable to the wagons used. The ordinary two and four mule wagon weighs about 1550 pounds and is known as an "escort wagon". This wagon is of the following dimensions: Body, 3 ft. 4 in. wide; 9 ft. 6 in. long; 1 ft. 9 in. high; capacity of body about 57 cubic feet; cover 3 ft. 4 in. wide, 8 ft. long; 3 ft. 6 in. deep; total capacity about 144 cubic feet. The following are the estimated weights ordinary, that should be considered as loads for wagons used upon marches. Two-mule wagons in addition to its weight, 1000 to 1200 pounds; Four-mule wagon in addition to its weight, 2000 to 2400 pounds; Six-mule "jerkline" wagon in addition to its weight, 2000 to 3300 pounds. While it is remarkable to the inexperienced cavalryman in the field to observe over what terrible country the American wheeled transportation can and does go, nevertheless there are times when it is imperative that all wagons, etc. be left behind and only pack-animals used with the troop.

The new mule is trained to lead, to herd, to keep with his own train, to stand quiet when being loaded or unloaded, to come quietly in to the picket line, and even to take his own place at the picket line between his mates, to follow the bell-mare everywhere, to allow himself to be caught whenever necessary, etc. The thorough training in the American Pack-trains is a revelation to those not familiar with packing. To train the mule well depends a good deal on the mule and a good deal on the patience and kindness of his trainer. Brutality is no more successful with the mule than with the cavalry horse. The daily allowance of forage for the pack-mule is 9 lb. of oats, corn, bran, or barley, and 14 lb. of hay. He is fed twice daily at the picket line, the feed being placed on the ground or on canvas feed covers, shelter-halves or gunny sacks. The morning feeding should be light if the train is to march, and the balance of the grain and all of the hay given at the evening feed after the camp is reached. The pack-mule should be liberally watered just before starting on the march and allowed to drink whenever opportunity offers during the march, care being taken that he is not too warm at the time, and especial care should be observed if the mule has been going at a rapid gait. What has been said about good water for the cavalry horse applies equally well to the mule in the pack-train. In camp the mule should be watered twice daily if kept in the picket-line and three times daily in hot weather. As the train is usually herded daily as long as work will allow, the herding ground should be near good running water, and the mules allowed free access to it at all times while out grazing. The pack-mule should be groomed at least once daily, and this thorough grooming should be given in the afternoon, after the work of the day is finished. In addition to this, the mule's back should be carefully brushed off in the morning, before putting on the "rigging", so as to avoid sores from dirt on the sides or back. The pack-mule, like the cavalry horse should never be washed. The pack-mule must at all times be shod all around. The shoes should be changed at least once a month, as with the cavalry horse, and the methods of shoeing are the same. Herding the pack-mules and allowing them to graze is practiced daily for the purpose of giving the animals plenty of good, green grass and if possible, good, running water and also for the purpose of training them to keep together, to follow the bell-mare and to come into and go out of the camp quietly and "in herd". Herding is one of the most important parts of the training as well as one of the most imperative parts of the feeding of the pack-animals and should be done daily whenever possible. This is also absolutely necessary for the pack-mule in order to keep the picket line clean and dry and fresh. When it becomes necessary on the march to cross rivers by swimming, the pack should be removed and sent across by other means. Only under the most imperative and unavoidable circumstances should an attempt ever be made to swim the pack-mule with his load on. As the load is very top-heavy the mule is apt to turn on his side and get drowned. The rigging may be left on when swimming the pack-mule; but if there be a good way to cross the riggings also, and time allows, these two should be removed and sent across, leaving the mules free to swim their best and saving the packing in the pads of the aparejo from getting wet. Pack-mules loaded should never be made to ford unknown or uncertain rivers until the ford has been carefully examined by sending several packers or troopers, mounted entirely across the stream first. These men should remain in plain sight at the landing place until all the mules have crossed.

Never should the train be pushed into a river to ford it if the depth be greater than 3½ feet and if the current is swift, this depth must be reduced to insure a successful passage of the train. As the mule heavily loaded is very liable to slip and drown if the bottom of the ford be rocky and slimy or too soft, the loads should be removed before they are sent into the water, and the loads afterward sent over by other means. Whenever crossing a river, either by swimming or fording, the bell-mare should first be sent across in front of the mules, as they will then follow her across with little difficulty if the ford is good. The bell-mare is a female horse, unsaddled, led by one of the packers mounted on his riding mule at the head of the train. The mare has a large metal bell suspended around her neck by a strap and the mules soon learn to follow her anywhere. This training is most important as it often happens that the bell-mare during dark nights or blinding blizzards is out of sight for several minutes at a time, and the train must follow the tinkle of the bell and thus keep together. The pack-mules soon learn to follow the bell, and after practice, little trouble is experienced in having the mules follow anywhere. For this reason the packer leading the bell-mare must always be careful to choose the best places, both across country or mountains and through timber or streams. The bell-mare should be specially chosen for her nerve, sense and strength, as an obstinate, easily frightened or physically weak one will prove of little or no value and will confuse the herd, often at the very worst places. All the packers are mounted on saddle mules, and these animals also must be well trained for their work. They must be bridle wise, tractable, strong and intelligent; agility is a prime requisite. They should be trained to stand still whenever the rider dismounts to readjust a loosened pack. By throwing the reins over the mule's head and allowing them to trail on the ground many saddle mules are taught to stand wherever left; others however are not so satisfactory, and if turned loose when the rider dismounts during the march, these will follow the pack mules up ahead and leave the rider to follow on foot. One method employed to make these mules stand wherever they are left is to bend the mule's head around toward his flank, usually the left one, and passing the reins over the mule's head, tie them together to the large horn or pommel of the saddle so as to keep the head thus turned. The mule in endeavoring to go forward, can only walk around and around on a small circle, and can easily be caught up again. Another way is to simply tie the mule to any convenient bush or tree by the reins. As the packer has frequently to dismount on the march to readjust loosened packs, to unpack a mule which has lain down with the pack on and cannot get up, and repack him after up, it is essential that his saddle mule be well trained. These saddle mules average about 14 hands in height and about 850 lb. and are required to fulfill the usual requirements for pack mules. On the march the train moves a short distance in rear of the troop to which attached. Troop pack trains are generally smaller than the regulation pack-train and usually have twelve pack mules and two or three packers on saddle mules. The train should not be so close as to crowd the rear horses of the troop at a halt or when temporarily delayed for a few moments, and yet should never be so far behind as to compel the troop to halt for it to catch up. Occasionally however it becomes impossible for the train to keep thus closed up on its troop at the more rapid gaits and as when crossing especially bad country. At such times a sufficient guard from the troop should be left to guard the train. Although the packers are frontiersmen generally and well armed, they are very busy readjusting the packs and looking after their mules and sudden surprise may overwhelm them. When marching the pack-master should lead the entire train, and the bell-mare should be led by another packer immediately behind the pack-master. The remainder of the packers should ride on the near side of the train and when the country is bad or the trail narrow, the packers riding on the side should distribute themselves *in* the train, each about five mules ahead or behind the nearest packer; at the rear of the train should ride the blacksmith and another packer. These men should keep the pack-animals closed up reasonably on the train, drive ahead any mule that may attempt to wander too far off the line of march and be ready quickly to dismount and readjust any pack that needs it. Under ordinary circumstances no effort should be made to keep the animals bunched, they soon acquire the habit on the march of going in single file and this should be allowed as it is the most satisfactory way. During the first few hours of marching, almost every pack will require readjustment, but after they have all been readjusted they will generally remain secure for the balance of the march unless some especially difficult country is encountered, or the gait unusually rapid. No time should be lost in dismounting and readjusting packs whenever necessary. One mile of travel with a loosened, sagging pack will do more to ruin a pack-mule than ten additional miles added on to the journey. The blinds should be distributed among the packers and used whenever a mule is being attended to. The pack-train must, except under extraordinary circumstances, be required to keep up with its troop; and this it will generally be able to do and for average daily marches of from twenty-five to thirty miles over fair country, no trouble will be experienced in keeping the train near the troop. It is wisest for the troop to regulate somewhat on its train as to gait so as to make it possible for the train to keep up without unduly tiring the mules. Leaving the train to come on by itself is always a bad practice. The march should not be made so long that the camp is reached after dark if it can be avoided; camp should be made early enough to allow the unloading of the mules quietly and allow for grazing for an hour or two before dark and for the grooming etc. Getting into camp with the troop after dark, and then having to wait several hours for the train to come up, will be found so disagreeable an experience after once tried, that whenever it can be done the train should be brought in at the same time. Thus supper is not delayed, time is allowed for arranging the packs and the riggings may be left on the mule's backs for fifteen or twenty minutes to allow for the gradual cooling of the backs, an essential point to remember. It is important that every cavalryman, whether officer or soldier, be reasonably expert in all that pertains to packing. Many times in field service the troopers will be needed to assist the packers in crossing the train over bad country or rivers or packers may be wholly lacking, when the troop will have to do its own, and if it is not well understood and carefully done the mules will soon be ruined. This training should be not merely in "throwing the diamond hitch" but to be good must embrace the setting up of the aparejo and rigging, keeping it in shape, knowing what to do in emergencies, how to put the rigging on, how to take it off, etc. This all requires much training and practice but its value will be quickly demonstrated when a troop is told to take a train and pack it and take the field!

The Cavalry Horse and His Pack
by J. J. Boniface (late 4th U.S. Cavalry).
Hudson-Kimberley, Kansas City, Mo. 1903.

Appendix II
Asses on Active Service[1]

THE donkey is for his size an excellent pack animal, and is so employed in many countries including India, Egypt, Somaliland, Persia, and China. His pace is slow, compared with the mule, and his load is only 100 lb. against 160 lb., but they demand comparatively little attention and small rations; they will do well on poor classes of forage and are valuable transport on lines of communication. In India they are, like mules, selected by measurement at not more than eight or less than three years of age.

Height	Girth	Rations
10 h. 2 in.	47 in.	Grain { Peace 3½ lb. If inferior, 5 lb. War 4 lb.
10 h. 1 in.	46 in.	Fodder, fresh 25 lb., dry, or Bhoosa, 13 lb.
10 h.h.	45 in.	Small donkeys get 3 to 4 lbs. grain,
9h. 3 in.	43 to 44 in.	20 lb. fresh fodder or 10 lb. dry.
9 h. 2 in.	41 to 42 in.	

They are particularly hardy and useful pack animals, if they are not overloaded or overdriven. Their pace is two and a half miles an hour, and they can cover 15 miles a day. (The ordinary distance of which mule transport is capable is 20 to 25 miles a day, carrying 160 lb. and the saddle; and this only when in good condition, if the rate is to be maintained for a considerable period.)

The saddle of pack donkeys is generally a pattern known as the "sunka". A "sunka" is a bolster stuffed with straw and supple sticks or canes, which is doubled in the centre, and its sides tied close together. The bend of the bolster is placed well in front of the animal's withers, so that these and the spines of the backbone lie in the space between the double portions, and on this the load is supported.

Both beneath and above the "sunka" a thick layer of blankets is

[1] This extract is reproduced by permission of the Director of Publications, Her Majesty's Stationery Office.

arranged to form a protective pad, and when in skilled hands it gives fairly good results. As, however, everything depends on the skill of the attendants in arranging this simple form of saddle, it is quite unsuited for transport which is not very thoroughly acquainted with it, and is in any case inferior to a good pack saddle of the right size.

(*Animal Management*, H.M.S.O., 1915)

Bibliography

THIS short list is meant to include only books in the English language which are not too hard to obtain, either new or secondhand. It does not include periodicals of any kind. Almost certainly the most useful literature on the donkey is in Spanish. One might, for example, cite R. Monner Sans: *Asnologia, Vocabulario y Refranero* (Buenos Aires, 1921), if only to give an airing to the splendid word 'Asnologia', which is a Castilian monopoly. So far as I know, no other tongue in Europe has a word with this meaning—"the science of all that pertains to donkeys."

Likewise the only book known to me on the ass in legend is G. Finzi, *L'Asino nelle Legende* (Turin, 1883), in another Mediterranean language. American books far outnumber British books in the English literature of the subject. Only books which explicitly or by implication mention the ass or the mule in their titles are included. I have made an exception, because of its importance, of Youatt, *The Horse*, but only on account of the special article on the Ass and Mule contributed by J. Skinner to the Philadelphia edition, and not to be found in any of the London editions. Many books on the horse contain chapters on the ass.

C. BANCROFT: *The Burros of Pairplay* (Boulder, Cal., 1968).

R. BORWICK: *People with Long Ears* (London, 1965).

—— *Donkeys* (London, 1970).

D. BROWER: *Going Light with Backpack and Burro* (Berkeley, Cal., 1970).

A. DENT and P. DAVIS: *Animals that Changed the World* (London, 1966).

M. DUNKELS: *Training your Donkey* (London, 1970).

W. HAGEL: *A Missourian and his Mule* (Kansas City, Mo., 1968).

W. G. LONG: *Asses v. Jackasses* (Portland, Oregon, 1969).

H. RILEY: *The Mule* (New York, 1867).

R. S. SUMMERHAYS: *The Donkey Owner's Guide* (London, 1970).

—— *Points and Type of the Donkey* (London, n.d.).

A. SWINFEN: *The Irish Donkey* (Cork, 1969).

W. TEGETMEIER and C. SUTHERLAND: *Horses, Asses, Zebras, and Mule-Breeding* (London, 1895).

H. WEIGHT: *Twenty-Mule Team Days in Death Valley* (Twentynine Palms, Cal., 1955).

M. DE WESSSELOW: *Donkeys, their Care and Management* (London, 1967).

W. YOUATT: *The Horse* (Philadelphia, 1845).

F. E. ZEUNER: *A History of Domesticated Animals* (London, 1963).

Index

compiled by S. Nicholls
(*page references to illustrations in italics*)

Wallfahrt nach Frantzösch [...]